THE
BOYS *of* '93

A trailblazer throughout his GAA career, in 1993 **Eamonn Coleman** became the first manager to lead Derry to All-Ireland success, a feat that remains his alone. Having taken over as manager in 1990, in 1992 he brought the county only its second National League title. At just 14 he became the youngest-ever player to win a senior club championship medal with his home team, Ballymaguigan; he was a member of Derry's first All-Ireland-winning minors in 1965 and All-Ireland U21 champions of 1968. He repeated his minor success as a manager, winning the All-Ireland in 1983. He died in June 2007 from non-Hodgkin's lymphoma.

Maria McCourt is Eamonn Coleman's niece and goddaughter. A former journalist and editor, she has worked as a news and sports reporter for publications in Ireland, Australia and the US. Maria started her career as a trainee journalist with the Belfast Media Group and went on to become editor of two of its newspapers, the *North Belfast News* and *South Belfast News*. The start-up editor of the national daily, *Daily Ireland*, in the late 2000s she led editorial teams in Cavan and Monaghan, establishing two weekly papers in the counties. She has also worked for the *Irish Echo* newspaper in Sydney and as a contributor for *Irish Echo* in New York.

THE
BOYS *of* '93
DERRY'S ALL-IRELAND KINGS

EAMONN COLEMAN
with Maria McCourt

Foreword by Joe Brolly

MERRION
PRESS

First published in 2018 by
Merrion Press
An imprint of Irish Academic Press
10 George's Street
Newbridge
Co. Kildare
Ireland
www.merrionpress.ie

9781785372179 (Paper)
9781785372186 (Kindle)
9781785372193 (Epub)
9781785372209 (PDF)

British Library Cataloguing in Publication Data
An entry can be found on request

Library of Congress Cataloging in Publication Data
An entry can be found on request

Interior design by www.jminfotechindia.com
Typeset in Minion Pro 11/15 pt
Printed and bound in the UK by TJ International Ltd.

Cover design by www.phoenix-graphicdesign.com

Front cover, top left: Henry Downey raises the Sam Maguire cup
for the first time in Derry's history. (Image courtesy of Sportsfile.)
Top right: Eamonn Coleman celebrating the semi-final win over
Dublin. (Image courtesy of Sportsfile.) Bottom: The starting fifteen
for Derry. (Image courtesy of Danny B. O'Kane.)

Back cover: Eamonn Coleman holds the Sam Maguire aloft.
(Image courtesy of *The Irish News*.)

For my mother, Mary McCourt, née Coleman (Mae).
With deepest love and gratitude.

Dedicated to the memory of Molly McCourt,
Willie Mulvenna Jnr and Janine McMullan.

Proceeds from the sale of this book will be
donated to cancer charities in Ireland.

CONTENTS

FOREWORD
by Joe Brolly

When we won the All-Ireland my father painted 'SAM 1993' across his oil tank in the yard. Every now and again, he touches it up. When the squad or a few of us meet up, it is always there, unspoken. We don't talk about the games, or who did what. We talk about the fun and the frolics. And we talk about Eamonn, who was the heart of the group.

'Wee men can't drink big pints,' he roared once at a team meeting, after Johnny McGurk, all 5' 6" of him, had said there was no harm in a few pints. 'I could drink big McGilligan under the table,' said Johnny. 'Could you fuck,' said McGilligan. Eamonn burst out laughing with the rest of us, and the temperance lecture broke up in confusion.

For a man who wasn't academic or well read, he was a superb orator with terrific emotional intelligence. In 1991, we beat Tyrone in a bad-tempered National League final. Seven days later, we met them in the first round of the Ulster championship in Celtic Park. The terraces were bulging. Coleman stood in the middle of the changing room, eyes blazing. Some players he left alone altogether. Others sometimes needed a perk up. 'Tony Scullion,' he said, shaking his head in disgust, 'wait to you hear what Mattie McGleenan said about you in the paper today.' He opened a newspaper and began to read what the young Tyrone forward had said about Tony. That he was surprised how lacking in pace Scullion was when he marked him in the league final. That he was over-rated. That he was done and that he would make sure he finished him off today. 'That's the respect he has for you Scullion, one of the greatest defenders ever to play the game. That's the respect he has for you,' he roared, shoving the paper into Scullion's face. Tony, normally mild-mannered, was enraged. He stood up, roared, and punched the door hard. We rumbled out onto the pitch like marines landing on the beach. Tony was superb in a total shut-out, never giving Mattie a kick.

Afterwards, when we had showered and were leaving, I spotted the paper, scrumpled up under the bench in the corner. I went over and lifted it. I read the interview, smiling and shaking my head. It was nothing only compliments from Mattie. A privilege to play against Tony Scullion and so on. Coleman had made it all up.

He once asked me to come over to the Rossa pitch in Magherafelt the Saturday before a championship match, but told me to say nothing about it. Patsy

O'Donnell and Eamonn's son Gary were there, already togged out. 'Jody', he said, 'I want you to test these two men out.' I went to full forward. First Patsy picked me up. Half a dozen times the ball was put in for me to run onto, take him on and try to score. Then it was Gary's turn. Afterwards, Eamonn beckoned me over to the sideline. 'Well Jody, which one of them would you pick at corner back tomorrow?' I thought about it for a second, and said, 'Have we nobody else?' He tried to keep a straight face, but quickly burst out laughing. 'What are we going to do with you, Jody?' he said, as he walked away, 'what are we going to do with you?'

In 1992, Donegal and ourselves were invited to a civic reception in the Guildhall to celebrate our National League title and their All-Ireland. We were all there, but Donegal sent their sub goalie. Coleman was livid, and viewed it as a deliberate insult. Before we played them in the Ulster Final the following year, he was delivering one of his blistering motivational speeches, not that it was needed. In the middle of it, he roared, 'That's how much they think of you. You're shit under their shoe. They sent the sub goalie to the reception in the Guildhall. Their fucking sub goalie.' Don Kelly, our sub goalie, put his hand up. 'What is it, Don?' 'I just wanted to say thanks a million, Eamonn.' The changing room, including Eamonn, exploded into laughter, yet another team meeting ending in confusion.

After we had won the All-Ireland, he invited one of the Biggs brothers into the panel. Gary and Gregory were good dual players and had been making a name for themselves. Biggs arrived for his first session, into this ultra-competitive, seasoned group of All-Ireland winners, led by Henry Downey, who would have intimidated Roy Keane. After the warm-up, we did ten 100m sprints. Then, it was into an A v B game. There was no sign of Biggs. Colm O'Kane, the groundsman, said, 'He went home after the sprints.' Coleman called Tohill over and said, 'Anthony, I think I brought the wrong wan.'

It is no exaggeration to say we loved the man. Maria McCourt's beautiful book captures a beautiful spirit, and for that we thank her.

NOTE TO THE READER

In early 2002, I got a call from Eamonn who asked, 'Have you ever thought about writing a book?'

'Just your autobiography,' I replied.

'Good. Meet me tomorrow night at the Carrickdale.'

Which I did along with Liam Hayes, the former Meath player and journalist. Eamonn was planning on retiring – again – and Liam was to publish his autobiography.

I agreed to write the book if Eamonn would agree to talk openly – having interviewed him as a sports journalist myself, I knew how cagey he could be.

He – unconvincingly – agreed and for the next few months we met, me having drawn up questions and him doing his best not to answer them: Derry and football were no bother, personal insights were a different matter.

The retirement was short-lived – again – and he called a halt in early summer, saying we'd return to the project when he eventually gave up the game.

NOTE TO THE READER

It was to be his cancer diagnosis in 2005 which brought us back to the idea, Eamonn suggesting we start again with 'just the two of us this time'.

I contacted several publishers and interest in the book was strong, unfortunately Eamonn wasn't and we got little else done.

It was a long time after his death before I could return to the tapes and longer still again before I knew what to do with them. He hadn't finished his story and I wasn't prepared to fill in the gaps.

Now, eleven years after his loss, and twenty-five since his greatest triumph, the autobiography we began has become a sports memoir of his All-Ireland glory.

The autobiographical elements remain, as does his incredible vernacular, the language of the lough shore which helped make his utterances so unforgettable. It would take a braver person than me to edit, 'Youse boys knows nathin' about futball', and when his speech conveyed so much, why would you even want to try? So, I've tried to stay true to his voice, just as I've stayed true to what he wanted to say, which is, basically, 'Derry and the 'Quigan rule' and 'the players is the men'. *Doire abu*.

PROLOGUE
SOME BOY
by Maria McCourt

Red, white. Silver. That's how I see it through his eyes as he leaves the shores of Lough Neagh. The red and white of Derry. The silver of the Sam Maguire. Blue, grey, green, black … red, white. Silver. The blue of the lough, the lane from his bungalow, up through the fields to the asphalt road. To Croke Park, boys … Croker. The silver of the Sam Maguire. The cathedral of Gaelic football awaits the 'third Sunday in September' faithful but today is just the third Saturday and the pilgrimage has yet to be made.

He is Eamonn Coleman, my uncle, my godfather and friend. But to them he's the Little General, the Boss, the Leader, the Man. For only the second time in the county's history – and the first in thirty-five years – the senior footballers are in the All-Ireland Final, the Championship's ultimate stage. By his side is his son Gary, a key player in this '93 team. The warm words from his aunt as he leaves: 'Don't come back here without Sam'. She's not renowned for her sentimentality, my grand aunt Eliza Bateson, but she has been here in their South Derry home since Eamonn was a boy.

'She came to look after the house when my mother was very ill. She did all the heavy work, for mammy was weak, ye know.' He tells me this during one of our chats. We're pals and I'm proud to be so. Possessed by football, at just thirteen, he had 'not a clue' how ill 'mammy' was. When she died – in the early summer of '61 – he missed her, 'Ach, I did surely but it was worse for Eileen and Mae.' Eileen is the eldest and his senior by nine years, then two years below her is Mae. She is my mother and despite being his big sister, she has always seemed, to all of us, the baby. 'They kissed her and touched her in the coffin but I couldn't. I didn't even cry.'

His father Tommy had little interest in the GAA but his mother was 'football mad'. He doesn't believe it's in the genes, though: 'All oul' nonsense that. Ye take football after nobody; you're either good enough or you're not.' So, the All-Ireland-winning Derry minor, and All-Ireland-winning U21, is now a successful county manager, in the final with his footballer son – his All-Ireland-winning Derry minor and Ulster U21-winning son.

On the surface, gruff and closed, he has 'no truck' with introspection and is famously a terror with sports journalists across Ireland. But, the more abuse he gives them the more their copy purrs. 'The High Priest of

Irreverence' is 'roguish', 'charismatic' and 'shrewd'. But Christ he can give them a lick – and anyone else should they rouse his ire. He's not bad tempered by any means, full of fun and craic and chat, but his passion for the game is messianic and there's no mercy – no mercy – for blasphemers.

'Youse boys knows nathin' about futball', he crowed to three unlucky scribes after his team hammered Down on the way to the Ulster Final, the crucial provincial landmark on their All-Ireland championship charge. Against the conquering Mournemen of '91, the nearly men of Derry hadn't a chance. 'Look at the scoreboard, boys. How could yis get it so wrong? Youse can't know anything about football, youse can't.' I know this – the country knows this – as they report their roasting post-match. Out of the sports pages the following day I can hear his voice rising on the 'can't', his South Derry brogue crackling in fury and triumph.

But seven weeks later I am at his side in Clones after Derry's Ulster Final win. In fact, I'm round his neck and his shoulder and his back, and we're up to our ankles in the mud of the pitch. I don't know how I got to him through the victory-crazed throng but we're jumping and hugging and shouting, delirious with delight. His sisters and my brothers are scattered all around but I'm off into the field and I reach him, just before the gathering press pack. 'Coleman', 'Eamonn', 'Eamonn, how does it feel to be Ulster champions?'

'Get away to fuck outta that will yis? Sure what do you want to talk to me for?'

And they fold with laughter, not with nervousness or embarrassment but with like, 'Ah here comes Coleman's craic', the elite of Ireland's sports writers facing this Ballymaguigan bricklayer. They soothe, cajole and coax, 'Ach Eamonn, now, come on', and I'm jostled back among the microphones, the jotters and the bustling pens. He'll give them what they need but first he'll give them hell.

'Why do they put up with you?' I ask as we relive the thunder of Clones. It's a few weeks after the game in my tiny north Belfast home. We're watching tapes of the great eighties Liverpool teams and talking about Brian Clough.

'Must be the nice smile, I have', turn of the head, flash, grin. He does that, he disarms you, devilment dancing from every pore, his smile is full frontal enamel and his green eyes wrinkle and spark. But on the sideline, he's a demon, pointing and effing and roaring. He's in front of the disciplinary committee so often, they tell him, 'Just take your usual seat.' But not this year, this year he has the best disciplinary record of any manager in Ireland because this year he has the best team. In the semi-final and five points down against the mighty Dubs, the roar of the Derry crowd lifts him out of his boots.

'Aw God man, it was tarra', he had thought, 'it'd be no good if we didn't win'.

I'd looked down the seats at my uncle, my mammy, my brothers, my aunt. They're ashen with fear and I pray to my Granda, dead since the November before, 'Ah Christ if you're there, Tommy, do something'. A committed non-believer, in desperation I'm a devotee. Derry get their miracle and my family praise the day.

One month later we're back in Croke Park for the All-Ireland Final against Cork. This time it's standing room only and I can see nothing through the heaving mass. On my tiptoes, I twist and stretch, smiling frantically at a harassed steward, 'Are there free seats around the ground anywhere?' Fifty All-Ireland Finals he's marshalled and someone always needs a better seat. 'See that dark-haired man down there?' I plead, 'That's my uncle Eamonn.'

He finds me a seat – among the Cork fans – and laughs, 'I hope you're as happy when you come out.'

I am. For the first time in 106 years Derry are All-Ireland kings and my uncle, my godfather and friend is the man to have them crowned. What a feat, what glory, what pride, I babble when I see him after the game. 'Bullshit this about managers', he says, 'the players is the men.'

The victors stay in Dublin for their gala celebration and we file off into the homeward-headed hordes. Out of the capital into Louth, we're the heroes along the way; the hunters home from the Hill. Kids fly makeshift Derry flags; we honk and beep horns in reply. On the steps of the convent in Drogheda, nuns wave cushion covers of red and white; across the border into Down and an elderly man flies a Supervalu bag, no doubt trailed from a kitchen drawer – the first red and white banner he could find. We know now that thirty-one counties have been at our backs all the way and as first-time winners of the Sam Maguire, they are letting us have our day.

For Eamonn, the next day's triumphant return proves to be more precious than the trophy he coveted: 'To come up through Tyrone with the Sam Maguire, I could've driv' up the street again.' We wait for hours in Maghera with the tens of thousands of others. Red and white. Then ... silver. As the victory bus inches towards us, Sam is the masthead at the front. We see Eamonn on the top deck, turn of the head, flash, grin. Then he's lost in a tumultuous sea as his boys carry him to the stage on their shoulders through the crowds and the crashing waves of unbridled joy. Not one for public speaking, we can hear little of him above the din except, 'We needed this All-Ireland more than Cork 'cos they already have six.' Red, white ... silver. It's all black and white to him.

But the elation soon fades to grey – he misses the training and the boys: 'You feel there should be more, you should have someone else to play. It's something you dream about all your life and then when you get it, your dream has gone.'

When the Championship of 1994 arrives, the All-Ireland champions are drawn to face Down. 'One of the best games of football ever played', he declares after Derry have lost their crown. For the first time in my life at a football match, I'd sank to my hunkers and cried. 'You never celebrate enough when you win the way you grieve when you lose': words of his I'd taken little notice of until that sunny day in May. He is more philosophical, although strangely cowed. 'We were spent; we'd got what we wanted. Down beat us in a brilliant game. It wasn't as sore as when we'd lost before for we knew we'd be back again.'

'I always get the dirty jobs', the county chairman whined as he sacked him. Just three months after that stunning game and Coleman was out the door. Men who he thought were his brothers-in-arms were still in and he was out. He had learned a bitter lesson. 'I'd have trusted them with my life.'

The coup was followed by a mutiny when his boys refused to play, wouldn't pull on the red and white or wear the Oak Leaf on their chests. Rumours spread throughout the country, speculation galore: 'He must have done something', 'Ye know Coleman', 'No smoke without fire'.

'Aye that's how they wanted it.' He's gutted, 'Saying nothing but letting all be said.' This is a side I've never seen to him – bewildered and betrayed. His squat fingers splay in emphasis, the scar on his lip snarling into his cheek.

'If they'd sacked me because I'd failed then, I'm a big boy, I could take it. But winning forty games from forty-seven, a National League and the All-Ireland, they couldn't come out and say that; they left a cloud of suspicion hanging over me.'

He challenged them in the press, to their faces and through the GAA. The National League kicked off and still his boys refused to play. Then he blew the final whistle on it. He knew when he'd been beat. 'If it was me, I'd go back', he told them, 'there's no one person bigger than Derry.' The officials won their battle but Derry lost the war, it's twenty-five years later and they've never come close again.

A decade after his sacking and the phone rings on my office desk. My older sister Bernadette asks, 'Can you come and sit with Eamonn?'

'There's not a trace of cancer in your body', the doctor had insisted but now she's on the phone telling me the doctor had been wrong.

'He's got non-Hodgkin's lymphoma, Maria.'
'Non-what? What's that? Lymphoma?'
'Yes.'

My brain scrambles to make sense of it. Non is no, which is a good thing, right? 'That's a good thing, right?'

'It's not good; it's cancer. Can you just come down? He wants me to go and tell Mae.'

Bernadette waits at the hospital and is standing stock still by his bedside when I arrive. He is upright in the bed, staring straight ahead. His eyes don't move towards me and there's a thickness in the room. I'm reminded of an explosion I got caught in as a schoolgirl; the bomb sucked the air out of the street. That's what it feels like here and I start to gabble to fill the void.

'The doctor will be round soon … We have to ask about your bloods … We need to find out who the consultant is … What does he think? What's the next move?'

He's had enough and snaps, 'The only thing we have to ask is am I gonna live or am I gonna die.' My mobile tolls in the vacuum. I leave the ward to take Bernadette's call. When I come back, he asks, 'How's Mae?' I nod gently, 'She's OK.' He knows that I am lying and then he starts to cry.

After the initial terror, the family machine flicks to 'on', through the chemo and the sickness, the waiting and then the reprieve. He takes a holiday to the US and gets engaged to his partner Colette.

'Engaged', I congratulate him, 'at your age, you fuckin' eejit?'

'I'm only fifty-eight. I'm thinking I might adopt a child.' Turn of the head, not quite a flash but he's still there with that brilliant grin.

Six months later, he feels lumps in his neck. 'Stem cell treatment', urge the doctors.

'What if it doesn't work?' asks Mae but I shush her in irritation. It's devastating what he's had to go through but it's not like he's going to die.

On a perfect June GAA Sunday, I go to Casement to watch our team. At half time the announcer asks us to pray for 'a great Derryman and Gael'. He's in the City Hospital just down the road where I'm heading after the game. I tell his partner, his children and his sisters how they chanted his name around the ground but none of it really matters now, and the following day he dies.

On Tuesday afternoon, as our family cars trail the hearse to South Derry, I notice a long line of cars filling the hard shoulder of the motorway. One by one they fall in behind us, the Oak Leaf county bringing him home. And for the next three days they descend; the mourners seem to pour from the skies. Over the brow of the hill they come, across the fields and down the lane. Minibuses are run from the clubhouse to his simple Loughshore home. The pitch where he was forged is now the car park for his wake. It's like his hallowed St Trea's grounds are paying homage to their most glittering prize, not the Sam Maguire but the local boy who brought him home: the man who carved a footnote for them in the history of the sport they were built to serve.

There's coaches from Cavan and Athlone; they come from Kerry, Cork and Down; there's Mercs with politicians and bigger Mercs with priests. There's one man in a wheelchair who has no time for football but for 'the man who, every Sunday, helped me into my car after Mass'. His club mates and his townland take his memory in their arms and they allow us as a family to feel, already, the legacy of the man. On the morning of the funeral, the club's youngsters line the lane and the boys of '93 lift him on their shoulders once again.

1 MIGHTY OAKS FROM LITTLE ACORNS GROW

It was November 1990. I'd been away from home and living in England for almost five years, having left for work in 1986 and staying after the break-up of my marriage. Approaching forty years of age and after sixteen years as a husband, I'd gone away to grow up.

Back home Fermanagh had beaten Derry in the first round of the McKenna Cup for the first time in Derry's history. The manager then had been Father Sean Hegarty. On my frequent trips home, I'd have given him a hand with the training but he had had enough. Now nobody would touch them with a bargepole.

I got a phone call to England. Harry Chivers, Chairman of the Derry County Board, spoke briefly on the phone. Would I be interested in taking the Derry job and if so would I fly over to meet him, the county secretary Patsy Mulholland and treasurer Jim McGuigan in the Archers Hotel in Magherafelt?

I flew home the following weekend. No interview took place; it was just, would I take the job with Mickey

Moran as trainer with me. I said I'd let them know. It wasn't the first time I'd been approached about the Derry senior job. Back in 1986, the then chairman Sean Bradley had asked me to take it on. I'd have taken the U21s of that year but the senior position wasn't the job I wanted.

My first move into county management had been three years earlier with the Derry minors and we'd gone on to win the All-Ireland of 1983. I'd then taken the U21 team of 1985 that nobody had wanted and we reached the All-Ireland Final only to be beaten by Cork. But I didn't get the U21 team whose backbone was the minors of '83. That was given to the senior management. I suppose they thought they would win an All-Ireland. They didn't.

That team in '86 would have been favourites to win the All-Ireland. Three years on from their minor championship, there was no reason they shouldn't have been kingpins of Ireland at U21 level. It was a waste of a team.

But in 1986 I wasn't prepared to take the seniors. They didn't have the players, I wasn't ready to do it and besides I needed to get away.

The years in England were the first I had spent away from home, away from Ireland. For the first time in my life I couldn't drive back to the shores of Lough Neagh. It bothered me going, bothered me leaving the lough, but I went and once I got there, I settled in well. But I was never away for more than three weeks at a time. Couldn't stick the Sundays in London, no football and nothing to do. I'd also made the conscious decision to come home regularly to see my daughter Margaret and my sons Gary and Vivian. We'd been through a lot and I didn't intend on losing the relationship we had built between us.

Now it was five years down the line and I'd the offer of the Derry senior job. It was time to think again.

It took me a week to decide. I discussed it with no one, not even Gary who was on the panel at the time. It was my decision. I felt they had the players and I was ready for the challenge. The independence I had learnt in England had made me bigger and bolder, stronger as a person and in my own opinions. I knew I could do the job.

'Improve the state of Derry football' was the only aim given to me and that's what I intended to do.

At that stage, Gary was already on the team having been brought in by Fr Hegarty after captaining Derry's All-Ireland-winning minors of 1989. Fr Hegarty had phoned me in England to tell me he was putting him on the panel and me, proud father and all as I am, advised him not to. Gary was light, he was only eighteen years of age and he wasn't a big strong fella but he was good enough so he came in.

Despite joining the senior panel for his county as I had done twenty-five years before, Gary had showed not the slightest bit of interest in football until he was around ten years old. In fact, it was my daughter Margaret who could be found on her own, kicking a ball for hours, almost from when she was fit to walk. Gary, on the other hand, couldn't have cared less. At a school match in Magherafelt one day, the ball went sailing over the hedge. As twenty-nine kids went scampering across the fields to find it, the bold Gary took the opportunity to sit down on the pitch for a rest.

But Margaret was the complete opposite, both off the pitch and on. A year older than Gary, she was determined not to let the fact that she was a girl get in the way of her playing football. Margaret was a brilliant footballer, very tough and bad-tempered, a dirty player actually.

Around 1983, I went to watch Magherafelt in an U10 final against Swatragh in Bellaghy. Both my son and my daughter were playing.

Margaret had cut her hair dead short so she could play on the team as a boy and even Damian Cassidy, who knew her well, didn't know she was at right half forward for the second half. They lost the game that day because they didn't start her. But even at that stage, I knew Gary was a bit special. I could see him thinking way ahead of the other kids and felt then he was good enough.

Vivian too had his share of footballing talent, winning an underage championship with Magherafelt and playing with the Derry minors before retiring at the grand old age of nineteen. It wasn't that the expectations were too much, or that his footballing career was bad, more a case of his social life being too good.

So, it was Gary who stuck with it and made the most of the talent he had. I never saw him as following in my footsteps – you can't take football after anyone. It's a help if you're in that environment but after that it's just how good you are in yourself.

He had grown in those years I was away but hadn't changed at all since he was a cub of fourteen. A bit bigger and bolder like myself, he was happy enough to have his da as manager but perhaps thought privately that it might make things hard for him.

I don't think either of us realised just how tough it would really be on him, or rather how tough I would turn out to be on him.

For years, Derry football had been in decline but at the start of the nineties, I could see the shoots of something there.

Adrian McGuckin had done great things with St Pat's in Maghera, winning the All-Ireland Senior Football Colleges championships in both '89 and '90. That, bolstered by the growth of St Pius' in Magherafelt, had meant the young boys coming through had already had their first taste of success with the schools.

At university level, St Mary's, Queen's and Jordanstown had got their hands on the Sigerson in '89, '90 and '91 and the success of the county minors of '89 had yet to be built upon.

As for me, I was ready to do the job. I felt I had something to prove, not to Gary as his da or manager or to anybody else for that matter. I only had to prove I was good enough to myself and I felt I was.

Starting with the minors had allowed me to learn and develop away from the pressure of attention. I'd say we were in the All-Ireland Final before we'd seen a county official at training so that had given us time to grow and learn together, the way we wanted, the way I wanted.

Now I had a belief in myself and the players; if that hadn't have been there, then I wouldn't have been there. If I hadn't thought I could do it better than everyone else that was there before me, I wouldn't have taken the job.

Even if I wasn't better than everybody else, I had to believe I was.

I came home out of England in February 1991 and things weren't very rosy. Mickey Moran had been looking after the training and, with my two selectors Dinny McKeever and Harry Gribben, operated from

October until the first three matches of the National League of 1991.

We'd won the first game of the league against Cavan in October but were beaten by Kildare and Antrim. We needed a win against Tyrone to have a chance of staying up.

I had moved home for that crucial game. Tyrone was never easy and with a young, up-and-coming team that included footballers of the class of Peter Canavan and Adrian Cush, who had already won at All-Ireland U21 level, we knew it was a tough one. But we got the victory at Celtic Park and another over Leitrim and then another at Longford where we hammered them off the park.

I called a meeting straight after the match in Slashers GAC in Longford. I had seen what I needed to see and it was time to introduce myself. My message was very simple: I am now in charge and if you want to be on this team, you have to train, you have to train when I tell you to train and you better put the county first. I knew we had the core of a good team in Derry. Some of the minors of '83 had already stood out, boys like Damien Cassidy, Dermot McNicholl and Johnny McGurk, and of the 1985 U21s, Enda Gormley was one to watch.

Their confidence was rock bottom. But I knew where we had to start. A bit of organisation, give them a system to play to and instil a tactical awareness.

There had been a lack of enthusiasm in Derry football through the years, a feeling that they couldn't expect any level of success never mind an All-Ireland. That had to change.

I had always had a good relationship with my players since winning the All-Ireland with the minors. I'd been at Kildress in County Tyrone but at county level, the Derry minor team of '83 was my stepping stone. I talked to them, explained what was needed so everyone could discuss what was happening and be a part of the overall effort. The night after training, I would have brought the forwards down to the house and we'd have watched tapes of the senior teams. We'd have took a bit from Kerry or from Meath and brought it into our own play, watched them and tried to develop them in training. And I was learning along with them – you're always learning. No matter how long you're there, everybody learns or they should do.

Since starting coaching, I got on well with players. Be straight with them and you'll get the best out of them – it was a simple enough philosophy. Having won two Sigersons back to back with Jordanstown in '85 and '86, I guess I had earned a reputation as a winner.

Fair and direct was the approach from the start and to let the players know I believed in them. They knew exactly how I approached the game and what I expected from them. That, to me, was crucial.

They hadn't been winning matches but once we started to put a run together they became more positive and assured in themselves. It spilled out. When you're winning with a team, even if you're not a great player, you start to believe you are better than you are. The belief and the commitment grew from there. The training which Mickey Moran put them through was tightening them up as well.

It hadn't been hard from me to settle into things as manager. Once I'd made up my mind to take on the team, it was just a matter of putting things into practice. I tried to build a family, every man playing for each other. Sometimes it works and sometimes it doesn't; like everything else it all depends on the players.

The family connection was important in Derry where we had four sets of brothers strengthening the team; Fergal P. and Damien McCusker, Henry and Seamus Downey, Johnny and Collie McGurk and Hugh Martin and Anthony Tohill. Then there was Gary and myself but for him it wasn't so much of a help.

Gary is any manager's treat: dedicated, hard-working and committed but when I came on the scene he was being judged as my son and not the great footballer he is.

Then there was me. People wouldn't believe it but I would be soft and at the start of my senior stint with

Derry, it was easier for me to pick on him because he was my son. I was sorer on him than anybody else. I could say things to him that maybe I should have been saying to another man in the dressing room and he bore the brunt of my tongue.

Mind you there was the odd time he more than deserved it. I had made a rule that the boys could play soccer but they weren't to be playing the Saturday before a Sunday game. Gary went and played for Newry Town ahead of a League game against Kildare in Ballinascreen. I knew about it, knew about it before he ever did it, but I never mentioned it. I gave him an awful eating before the game on Sunday. I don't think another man would have sat and took it and I wouldn't let him tog out.

The wind and the rain was that bad that day, that what little crowd there was was in the stands. Kildare wouldn't keep a ball behind the net because they were trying to slow the game down. I made him go out and stand behind the goals and every time the ball went over the wire he'd to go and get it back. He came in drenched. That put an end to Gary's soccer. I could maybe even understand someone else going and playing, but Gary?

It was hard on him. I was hard on him and it took me a few years to learn that I had to treat him like everybody else. I suppose there was the fear that people would accuse me of singling him out for special attention because of who he was. I did but not in the way everyone expected.

And he had no escape. The rest of them could go home and mouth me off to high heaven. He had to look at me again. But he's a quiet boy and said nothing. He stayed a player on the field and a son when we were at home. I eventually learned how to separate being his manager and his da and that if things weren't going well I couldn't take it out on him.

The team started coming together during the league of '91. We put together a run of wins – which eventually stretched to sixteen – and the boys began believing in their ability.

My first championship game in charge was a preliminary against Tyrone in Omagh. The Red Hands looked like winners all the way until Damian Cassidy scored a goal in the dying minutes to send us through to meet Down in the championship first round proper.

It was the first of some mighty clashes with Down who we met at the Athletic Grounds in Armagh.

Anthony Tohill had come home out of Australia the Wednesday before the game and made his debut that day at midfield. Both he and Brian McGilligan showed us what was possible after Greg Blayney was given the line. Having been five points down at half time, we fought our way back into it only for Ross Carr to force the replay with the last kick of the game. Down beat us in the replay and went on to win the All-Ireland. That was a special moment. We felt we had pushed Down to the limit and if they could win an All-Ireland then we were very close.

Disappointed that we hadn't beaten them, we approached the National League of '92 with all guns blazing. The stall was set out; we were going to win the League, which we did for the first time since 1947, the year I was born, beating a very fancied Tyrone team in the final at Croke Park. We played badly in the National League final and should have been beat but got a very lucky goal. But on those occasions, it doesn't matter how you win as long as you win.

The wave of enthusiasm I felt had been lacking in Derry for so long had started to roll through the county. Watching Derry teams play before I was involved, I felt that they never believed they could win an All-Ireland. Now people wanted to play for Derry, we were winning games, everybody wanted to train and the family was getting stronger. The hype was high and so were the expectations.

We couldn't wait to get at the '92 Championship and two weeks after that final, we played Tyrone again, this time at Celtic Park, and gave a definite answer that day. We beat them by five points but we were superior all through. Only that Gary scored an own goal, we would have won much easier. It wasn't his fault – the ball bounced out of him and there was nothing he could do about it so he escaped an eating that day.

Next, we played Monaghan in Castleblayney and after being nine points ahead at half time, Monaghan came storming back into it, needing Declan Bateson to score us a goal in the dying seconds to draw the game. We beat them in the replay in Derry city by seven points.

When the semi-final draw threw up Down, boys we were chomping at the bit. The big meeting at Casement Park – that was the one we wanted, the big clash everyone was waiting on. The All-Ireland and Ulster champions of Down and the National League champions of Derry. Derry had been unbeaten since the previous year's Championship defeat to Down and we approached the game like it was an Ulster Final.

A tremendous amount of work was being put in by the players and management. We were training three nights a week and the management team met another night, talking about the games and how the players performed. Everyone knew where we wanted to go and we were pulling in the one direction.

Pete McGrath's men had gone to Croke Park in '91 and smashed any notion that Ulster teams were there just for a day out. If they could do it then we were a stone's throw from it and we intended to give a definite answer that day in Casement Park.

We laid out our intentions, beating Down by four points in a great game of football where we were by far the better team. A team that included Mickey Linden, Greg Blayney, D.J. Kane and James McCartan was well fancied for another All-Ireland and well fancied to beat us in Belfast. They didn't and I knew we were on our way.

I wasn't the only one who was fooled that year. For almost an hour after the game, the Derry supporters stood in the stands chanting 'We want Sam'.

After seeing to Down, I believed we could give them what they wanted. For us, Down was the team to beat but we had forgotten they weren't the only team to beat to reach the road to Croke Park.

Donegal had gone about their business amidst all the talk of Derry and Down and quietly arrived in the final from the other side of the draw, beating Fermanagh and Tyrone. Brian McEniff must have been a very happy man watching our celebrations from the stands in Casement Park that day.

Defeat to Meath in the All-Ireland Semi-Final of 1988 had hung a cloud over Donegal but they had learned something that at that stage I hadn't.

In my reckoning, the Donegal team of '92 had come late; they should have achieved something before 1992. The team of 1988 was a great bunch of players but they took a couple more years to learn than they should have and were coming down off the peak. Like Derry, they could have won more than they did.

It wasn't that we had underestimated Donegal but we had already achieved our ambition. After waiting a year to play Down everything had been focussed on them and unbeknownst to ourselves, we started to ease off.

Naivety and inexperience allowed us to get caught up in the occasion; we had started to believe the hype and it proved to be our downfall. Donegal had learnt that lesson before and were determined not to fall to it again.

In 1992, my whole life was taken up by football: four nights a week running to football, Sundays going to watch other county teams you'd have a chance of meeting and it was important for me to be back home with Gary and Vivian after being away. Margaret was coming home for the matches from England, where she'd gone to study, and life was very good.

Then, on a sunny day in Clones, Donegal took the Ulster title that I felt in my gut would be ours and I tasted the bitterest disappointment of my entire footballing life.

Looking back now, we just weren't ready, weren't mature enough but I thought I never would get over it. In football, defeat lingers much longer than victory, on and on and on. The celebration of winning never outdoes the devastation of losing. I was sick.

Returning home to the lough, I'd say I didn't go out for a month. I never crossed the door for I couldn't bear to speak about it. The last thing I thought about going to bed at night was the 'what ifs' and the 'whys'. The mornings weren't any better as the disappointment filled my head as soon as I awoke. It was that much, that bad and I swore I'd learnt a lesson I would never forget.

Waiting back at the lough after that bitter defeat was my father, Tommy Coleman, and my aunt, Eliza Bateson, who had come to look after the house after the death of my mother Peggy when I was thirteen.

Eliza, like my mother, would have argued the day long about football but my father was never a big man for it and would usually have had more kop on. He knew if I came home on the losing side I would be in bad form so said nothing. But the disappointment wasn't just on me that day.

'You may forget about Derry', he said when I walked in, 'Sam Maguire will never be in this house'.

He was wrong. Just over a year later Sam Maguire was there but my father wasn't.

The most passionate my da ever got about football was when he was watching Tyrone. He never told me why but he hated them with a passion, him who was born in the county and whose mother and father are buried at the Old Cross in Ardboe.

He was a good father, but strict. If he said it was to be done this way, it was done that way and no argument about it.

He had worked as a farm labourer in and around Derry and Tyrone but wages were small and he was always at something else so he could get my mother what she needed for the house, for my sisters and me.

A precise and tidy man in everything he did, he took a massive stroke in November of '92 whilst straightening a hospital bed that wasn't made to his liking.

He had gone into the Mid Ulster Hospital after suffering his thirteenth heart attack, the first of which had struck him back in 1968.

Disciplined and meticulous, he would follow the doctor's orders to the letter and kept his small but strong frame healthy despite the many heart scares.

The National League had started again in October and I was desperate to get rid of the ghost of the Ulster Final defeat. The only way I knew how was through football and after the long summer, life was thankfully once more a whirl of football training and meetings.

I had been into the hospital to see him on the Friday night, as we were due in Limerick for a League game on Sunday. At around seven o'clock on the Saturday morning, I got a call to the house: 'Your father's not well; you'd better come in'.

He never spoke again after the stroke and died the following Thursday.

My da was eighty-two and had a good life. I missed him but not in the way I had missed my mother.

We had had a good relationship but nothing compared to the relationship me and Gary would have. In those days you didn't speak to your father about everyday life and children were more afraid of their parents. By the time Margaret, Gary and Vivian were growing up, all that had changed; mothers and fathers were more open and so were kids. I'm closer to my kids than he was but that was the way of his generation more than anything else.

His strict and disciplined ways maybe come out of me in the dressing room but then I can go home and be the da that I am to my children. But he was gone and I, like the rest of us, had to get on. It had been a tough few years, filled with expectation and hope but eventually made of defeat and loss.

There had to be something else.

2 'YOUSE BOYS KNOWS NATHIN' ABOUT FUTBALL'

I stood in the dressing room in the Marshes in Newry. May of '93. The talking was all done and I had little left to say.

'This is it, boys. I have nothing more to give yez. This is all I've got. We have to do it today.'

Damien Barton got to his feet, shoved out his chest, 'Let's go now, boys. It's time to deliver.'

And deliver they did, a killer start to our All-Ireland campaign – the Massacre at the Marshes. Nobody had given us a chance at the start of the Championship in 1993 after a defeat in the League at the hands of Donegal.

Every game between us and our neighbouring county then was a real battle, in a football sense and in every other way. The National League quarter-final on Easter Day wasn't any different. Kieran McKeever was sent off for breaking Tommy Ryan's jaw and from a brilliant first half in which Derry were superior, Donegal came late to beat us by a point.

After the match, the Donegal players stood up on the wire to their crowd in celebration but if people had looked closely at Derry they'd have seen; we didn't go out to get beat but the League wasn't a priority. We had won the League the year before and we were training very, very hard for the Championship. Anybody who was there that had have looked closely at the first thirty-five minutes would have seen Derry were by far the better team. We were playing brilliant football but with the heavy training we completely tired in the last twenty minutes. Gary was playing centre half back that day at twenty years of age on Martin McHugh and played very well but we hadn't Tony Scullion. We'd a few other players missing too and Kieran McKeever sent off. Although we were beaten, I knew things were going well.

The lessons of '92 had learned me and I swore I'd never forget how sick I was at getting deflected coming up to the Ulster Final against Donegal. It's not that we'd underestimated the men from the hills but Down were the All-Ireland champions and we had waited a year to play them.

McEniff's men knew in their guts that we were snapping at the heels of their Ulster title and when they climbed the wire to their supporters, shaking their fists in triumph, they weren't the only boys shaking their fists that day.

There was no love lost between Derry and Donegal and that aggression wasn't just confined to the players. After the game in Breffni Park, the Derry treasurer,

Jim McGuigan, got involved in the tunnel, slabberin with McEniff. No blows were exchanged between th two but they were flying everywhere else.

Later in the Hillgrove Hotel, when McKeevei walked in for his meal along with Damien Barton the entire Donegal team got to their feet. Chairs clattered back as the Derry team rose as one, ready for another row, but with some sensible interventions from Brian McEniff and myself and a lot of 'Now, now fellas', it was kept for the field at Clones and the Ulster Final.

After that League defeat, it was all Down, Down, Down – these journalists and sports writers who knows frig all about football most of them.

If they'd have sat down and looked at that game, they would have seen a Derry team that was really on the up, playing superb football in the first half but tired by the heavy training in the build up to the Championship – a Derry team who hadn't gone out to get beat but one that had won the League the year before and now had bigger fish to fry.

Dickheads, most of them – haven't got a clue. 'Do you think you'll win?' Anybody thinks they're not going to win shouldn't be on the bus. If I was a journalist, I wouldn't ask things like that; I'd look at the team and make an assessment myself and know that everybody goes out to win but then you have to look deeper. I learnt only to tell them what I wanted

them to know and if they want to believe it, it's alright. There's a few boys might know their football but there's some would definitely sink you.

I'd had a lash at one or two of them a few times before but they kept coming back for more – must be the nice smile I have. But nobody really gave us a chance and Down were tipped for the match.

But Derry football had changed. I had tried to base a style around the best of Donegal and Meath, who both held possession of the ball. Meath were big and strong like ourselves – with the exception of wee Johnny McGurk. Donegal didn't kick the ball away. Our theme, like theirs, was to keep possession. When we had the ball, the other team hadn't got it; it was as simple as that. That's what we preached, that's what we stuck to and that's why we started winning.

Despite the criticisms in the media, my own confidence didn't need any boosting as we started off the Championship. I had been convinced that we could win an All-Ireland in '92 but when I look back, I realise we just weren't ready. We had moved on another step in '93 and the balls we were kicking away in '92, we just weren't doing that anymore. We were holding on and we'd learnt not to panic. Gary, Tohill and Declan Bateson and boys like that had also matured; we had grown up as a unit and we were starting our third year together as a fairly settled team. In '93, every game was

The Derry All-Ireland minor winning team of 1965 in which Eamonn featured. Standing first from left is Derry scoring legend Sean O'Connell and second from right, Fr Seamus Shields, two huge influences on a young Eamonn pictured third from left, front row.

Eamonn's son Gary followed in his father's footsteps by winning an All-Ireland minor title with his county, captaining the winning team in 1989.

Eamonn with Gary after taking over the management role. Gary was already on the county panel after being brought in by the previous manager, Father Sean Hegarty.

Eamonn walks the pitch at his beloved St Trea's, Ballymaguigan, with whom at 14 years old he became the youngest ever player to win a senior county championship medal.

Also pictured at the Ballymaguigan pitch, Eamonn with members of his background team: trainer Mickey Moran, selector Harry Gribben and physio Sean Moran.

Henry Downey lifting the National League trophy in 1992. The first silverware won under Eamonn's management, the National League victory was only the second in Derry's history, the first in 1947, the year Eamonn was born.

Damian Barton is tackled by Brian Burns during the 3-11 to 0-9 defeat of Down in Newry in May 1993 which led to the 'Massacre at the Marshes' tag.

Referee Tommy Sugrue pays close attention to D.J. Kane's challenge on Enda Gormley during the Ulster Quarter-Final in Newry.

Dermot Heaney beats Monaghan's Eugene Sherry to the ball in the Ulster Semi-Final on 20 June at Casement Park.

Water splashes around Fergal McCusker as he skids away from Donegal's Paul Carr in the Ulster Final at Clones on July 18.

Anthony Tohill holds off the Donegal challenge in a rain-sodden Clones.

Brian McGilligan goes in for the ball against Donegal's Mark Crossan at Clones.

Dermot McNicholl strikes the ball as the rain continues to pour.

Captain Henry Downey lifting the Anglo Celt Cup, 1993. Among the crowd to Henry's right is Bishop of Derry Edward Daly and to his left, future GAA president Sean McCague. (Image courtesy of Sportsfile.)

Anthony Tohill slips past Dublin midfielder Paul Bealin in the All Ireland Semi-Final at Croke Park on 22 August.

Joe Brolly torments the Dublin defence.

Gary Coleman on his way to scoring a point against Dublin in the semi-final.

An emotional Eamonn on the Croke Park pitch celebrating the semi-final win over Dublin. (Image courtesy of Sportsfile.)

'92's semi-final against Down; it didn't matter who we were playing.

There was pressure as ever but I genuinely felt we were the best team in the country. I didn't feel I was the best manager in the country, couldn't say I was the best manager in the country; I had never won an All-Ireland.

But that solid belief in the players I had in front of me had made me calmer and for a man who likes to have his say to the odd referee, I'd the best disciplinary record of any manager in the country that year. I was also well aware it was my last shot at Sam.

On the road to the Marshes that day, a group of Derry supporters had gathered at a petrol station and struck up a conversation with a member of the county board.

Talk of the match ended with his statement: 'We'll get beat today but at least we'll get rid of Coleman.'

I hadn't felt the vultures circling. I didn't give a damn about people who thought the success of the county should focus on them and not the players. The players is the men and anyone who says different is simple. But I felt in myself we had to do it that year, not because I was out to save my own skin but because I expected it of myself. I was going into my third year and yes, we'd won the League, we had 'improved the state of Derry football' but we hadn't got Sam.

But the nervousness before a big Championship game was different that day in Newry; it felt more like a time of reckoning. This is where we would be judged and in those final minutes before the throw in, I did the only thing any manager can do and handed it over to the ones that really matter.

There's always a risk of overkill in those vital minutes before a big game. As a manager, the trick is knowing when you're treading the line. There are times when you need to be forceful and others when you lead by friendship. This was one of those times when I had to say, 'It's your turn, boys. The pressure's on you but, at the end of the day, win or lose, I'm the one that takes the rap and I'm behind you all the way.'

I never had any doubt but that we would beat Down but never imagined we would beat them by eleven points. We had the beating of them by maybe six or seven but the hardy men from the Mournes caved in.

Boys, they hated that as much as I enjoyed it. A manager from the Ulster Bank who sponsored Down at that time stopped me on the way out of the ground. 'Coleman, you'll not be content 'til you bankrupt us'. I'd have bankrupted Ireland for Sam.

We had gone into the match without two of our best defenders in McKeever, and Tony Scullion who had picked up an ankle injury in an oul' league match against Louth, had to be taken off after fifteen minutes. Linden, as ever, was going well.

But Down must have thought we were pure stupid. Danny Quinn, a big man, was at full back and they put James McCartan into full forward, like I was going to leave that wee, small quick boy on Quinn. Another wee small quick boy, Johnny McGurk, was moved onto McCartan. Tohill was, ach, just Tohill in the middle of the field and we walked away with a 3-11 to 0-9 victory. In the scheme of things, it didn't matter. It was just the first hurdle and there'd be more to be gotten over.

But the Scullion injury was a blow. Tony had been out for ten weeks but he was just lacking that sharpness. The team trained in Ballymaguigan the Saturday after the Down game and the people along the line were all, 'Scullion's finished. Scullion's done'.

The man hadn't been playing, just wasn't ready, but that week he trained every night on his own as well as with us. He did it to get himself fit; he knew himself the match fitness just wasn't there yet, so he put in the work: commitment and dedication. It's part of him. When he came back, you'd have thought he had never been away from us. He gave an exhibition and he never looked back. A proud man from a proud people, Tony Scullion went on to have his greatest year in 1993 but, of course, the so-called experts didn't see it.

Like the unequal celebration of victory against the disappointment of defeat, a player will never get the praise he deserves in the amounts he'll get of criticism. One bad game in three years, that's the one they'll remember. That's people in general but definitely some Derry people.

As for the managers, well, GAA managers is pure simple. There's no other way to put it.

To be doing this job that takes up your whole life and to be taking the stick that you take, to have people criticise you from a height that nine times out of ten hasn't the baldiest idea between a good footballer and a bad footballer – managers get far too much credit and they get far too much stick. I made that point to these genius sports reporters who, all of a sudden, wanted to know about us after the Down game.

'What do you want to talk to me for?' I said. 'Sure, Derry's no good – Derry haven't got a chance. Go on and get away with yez. Youse boys knows nathin' about futball.' Ahh, they took it well enough.

But they nor nobody else outside of a football field was on my mind as we met Monaghan at Casement Park. Down was one big hurdle out of the way and we weren't going to go overboard about beating them and not look out for Monaghan or anybody else.

With fourteen minutes to go at Casement Park, it was a drawn game. We sent in Joe Brolly and Brian

McCormick. Brolly scored three points, McCormick got one and Enda Gormley notched up seven to send us through, winning by eight points. Back to where we were the year before, back in the Ulster Final.

Everything that year had led up to the titanic battle between Derry and Donegal. That was the one we all wanted after the tension at the League match that almost spilled over into a major row as well as a run-in with their supporters at the replayed match between Armagh and Donegal which sent Donegal through to the final.

We had been away for the weekend, playing Mayo, and had come back to Cavan to watch the game at Breffni. Boys, the stick we took walking along the line that day from the Donegal crowd was something else. Henry Downey and I were together and were given some special treatment, getting hit with all the trash of the day. We didn't need our resolve hardened but it never did us a bit of harm leading up to the final on 18 July.

The Ulster Final of 1993 should never have been played after it lashed all day at Clones but I'm convinced the wet day saved Donegal from a terrible, mighty hammering. People said the wet day suited Derry, but I've said it all along, we'd have slaughtered them in dry conditions. It wasn't that it was mucky but by Jesus it was wet with water lying all over the pitch.

People says big players play well in heavy conditions. I don't agree. Big players find it very hard to keep their balance in heavy conditions and small men's better balanced. The bad day saved Donegal from a tanking.

Myself and Brian McEniff was standing outside before the teams came out, both in agreement that it shouldn't go ahead. There wasn't a steward to be seen. I know when you go to Clones to play, all the officials of the day is there, letting you in and directing you where to go. Nobody wanted to see us because they knew it shouldn't have been played. I'd have been delighted for it to be called off; it was dangerous. Derry had a minor player broke his leg that day but the crowd was there and they were afraid of losing the money. We couldn't ask them to call it off for we saw nobody; the only one we saw was the referee and he said he saw nobody either.

So, there was nothing else said between us, no mind games at that stage. If you start then, you're only fooling yourself. Like two boxers coming to the ring, the plan is already set; there's no point threatening the other from the dressing room.

I rated Donegal a very good team, as good as Down, but we always felt it harder to beat Donegal. They held the ball up and made it do all the work, which meant we were always chasing it down.

It was a tough match in tough conditions. Just before half time, Donegal got a point to go one up, 0-5 to 0-4. Henry Downey couldn't get tackling the man that scored the point, with Martin McHugh hauling him back by the jersey. Coming off at half time, I pulled the referee, Tommy McDermott: 'You saw McHugh holding. That shouldn't have been a point'. A passing James McHugh remarked, 'Aw Eamonn, where's your All-Ireland medals?'

We had changed the team before the match. Mícheál Ó Muircheartaigh had came into the dressing room and asked me was there any changes. I said no but we had dropped Danny Quinn and threw Tony Scullion to full back and had Gary at corner back on Declan Bonner. Gary had been having an outstanding game against him and Bonner was eventually taken off. James McHugh was moved in on him but he was substituted too. As he passed me on the line I couldn't resist a swipe. 'I think, James, there's no chance of one of those All-Ireland medals you're so fond of talking about this year.'

Myself and McEniff also stayed true to form, jabbing away at each other. Pete McGrath and myself would never have had a cross word but with Brian it was different, me and him rubbing each other up the wrong way, but when the match was over, it was over.

During the game he had had words with Gormley. I told him to 'Fuck off'.

'I'd do anything to win, Eamonn', he replied, which is fair enough. But near the end of the game, he almost started a riot. At the far side of the pitch, things had been bubbling with the Donegal corner forward Manus Boyle and Kieran McKeever. McEniff took off across the pitch, incensing the Derry support; some of them tried to get over the wire at him. They'd only scored one point in the second half; he knew we had them pinned back, on the cuff and that the Anglo Celt wasn't heading for the hills that year.

The week after the Ulster Final, I spent a few hours with McEniff at his hotel in Donegal but you're inclined not to talk too much football with a man whose Ulster title you've just taken away and whose All-Ireland crown you're after for yourself. And, being the perfect gentleman that I am, I didn't mention it to him at the time but I was one happy person.

Beating Donegal in Clones to win the Ulster championship was a sweet victory. The sweetest. Winning the All-Ireland was brilliant but beating Donegal in Clones that day was as sweet as the defeat had been terrible the year before – the one and only time it ever equalled out. It was brilliant coming home on the bus. Brilliant that night too – the journey from Clones, celebrating with the players. We continued celebrating Derry's first Ulster championship since 1987 in Maghera the Monday and Tuesday before getting back to training on Thursday.

At home, the whole family was delighted for myself, for the team and for Gary. I had never stopped to think to myself, 'That's my son out there', during the Ulster Final. I had stopped to think, 'You'd better play well'. Being together in victory didn't bring us any closer; you're as close as you can be father and son, but I was proud that he was part of it. But getting our hands on the Anglo Celt, it was solid proof that we were Championship contenders and the more the players believed that, the easier my job would be.

3 'THE PLAYERS IS THE MEN'

The build up to the All-Ireland Semi-Final was something special. Mickey Moran's training was excellent and no matter what you asked of the players, they did it, and no matter when you called training, the entire panel turned up. The spirit was great but we were concerned about Dublin naturally. You've always got to be concerned about the Leinster champions and at that stage, Dublin had won their second of what would be four Leinster titles in a row.

Other worries that should never have been bothering us at anytime, never mind in the weeks before such a mighty clash, reared up after a challenge game at Ballinlough GFC in Meath.

After travelling down to play Meath in a challenge match, I had asked Colm O'Rourke to have a word with the team about the Dublin game. A great player and a man who had a lot of experience of Croke Park, he spoke of what to expect, what an All-Ireland Semi-Final meant and about the importance of the team – the whole team – in winning Sam.

Sitting down for a meal in the hotel afterwards and after that great talk on team spirit, the Derry treasurer

Jim McGuigan reached across the table and smacked our captain, Henry Downey, in the face.

I hadn't seen the punch being thrown but Jesus there was going to be a racket. Trying to restrain Downey, I insisted he would do no good by striking back.

'Have sense, Henry. You hit him and they'll say one's as bad as the other. Don't hit him and they'll have to deal with it.'

The row had broken out over tracksuits for the players. Downey had arranged to get boots for the boys and was asking McGuigan as treasurer to sort out gear. Pissed off that McGuigan didn't seem prepared to sort it out, Downey had made some craic or other: 'Fuck sake, Jim, you're only the county's treasurer; it's not your money we're after.'

That's how it started and although I'd no way of knowing it, that punch was a sucker blow for me. After the meal was finished, unbeknownst to me, Henry called in the guards.

They arrived after I had left for home and spoke to McGuigan in the car. No charges were made and as far as I was concerned, that was that. But in the tiny world of GAA, the word had got out and the next day I got a call from Mick Dunne of the Irish Independent.

'I hear, Eamonn, you'd some bother in the dressing rooms after the Meath game yesterday – that a player was struck by a member of the county board.'

He had it right but for where it took place. 'I don't know where you get your information from', I said. 'It's the first I heard of it and I was the last man to leave the changing rooms.' It never hit the papers.

At training that Tuesday, the county chairman Harry Chivers phoned me to thank me for the way I had handled the situation with the press. He finished by assuring me the board would deal with McGuigan.

They didn't, so the players decided to take action themselves. Their view was that this man had hit their captain and they weren't prepared to let it go at that. If the county board had even suspended him for a month, two weeks even, it would have been done, forgotten about, but it didn't happen so it went on.

Jim McGuigan had been the Derry county treasurer since 1964 and was the only one that ever really travelled on the bus with the players and the management team. The players took a vote that he wouldn't be allowed on the bus on the trip to Dublin for the semi-final. It was the players' decision, nothing do with me. Besides, I had more important things on my mind – trying to get a team ready for one of the biggest game of their lives.

In '93, from the Ulster Semi-Final, we knew the team we really wanted but we didn't get it out on the field, I would say, until that All-Ireland Semi-Final.

We couldn't wait for it, couldn't wait to get at the Dubs. The team was ready, the management was ready and we felt that this was going to be our year.

Dublin was a big, strong, tough team with Dr Pat O'Neill at the helm and they carried the favourites tag going into Croke Park. Coming from Ulster, there was a time not long passed when we were only supposed to go to Croke Park and play well. We weren't supposed to win – that belonged to the twenty-six counties. But Down's great breakthrough in '91 had laid the foundation for everybody: Donegal, Derry, Tyrone and the rest. Everybody believed then, and it's been the same since, when Ulster teams go to Croke Park, we've as good a chance as anybody.

Dublin themselves had been beaten the year before in the All-Ireland Final by Donegal, so that thing specifically about the Dubs in Croke Park had been smashed too. We respected Dublin but we'd no fear of them because we truly believed we could beat anybody, no matter who they were, and if we were behind we would come back and win. It comes from winning and beating the good teams, which we'd done all the way to Croke Park. Derry had come from nowhere to be a force in Ireland. We'd gone sixteen games, two years at that time, and only been beaten in one National League match and lost one championship match. We weren't going to Dublin for the Northerners' big day out.

Myself and Henry intended on getting that message across before a ball had been touched and decided to break away from the Hill on the pre-match parade, the first time a team would have done that. We weren't going to go past the Hill and have the Dublin crowd abusing the Derry team. We were going to show them, 'We don't worry about you Dubs or anybody else and we'll not be intimidated by the fearsome Hill 16.'

For me, it was the greatest game of the Championship, probably one of the best games of football we played; Derry had one outstanding second half. We got the rub of the green alright but we made it for ourselves after trailing 0-4 to 0-9 at half time.

The normally timid Mickey Moran got cross during the break, one of the few times I ever saw him angry. He put it up to the team: 'Are you going to be like every other Derry team, coming here just to show well, then dropping your heads and letting it get away from you?' And Henry Downey, being the tremendous captain that he was, urged them to make a pact, that they weren't going to be beaten.

The roar of the Derry crowd as we came out onto the pitch for the second half would have lifted you off your boots. We were five points behind but Derry pushed it all the way and within a minute and a half, there was three in it.

With ten minutes to go there was still three in it until Dublin went up and scored again. Straight from the kick out we'd a four-man move and scored. Immediately Dublin attacked but Scullion got the ball;

seven Derry men handled it and there wasn't another Dublin mitt on it until John O'Leary was kicking it out at the other end to take us within two points.

I knew then we had it. Dublin started to buckle, started looking at each other, blaming the men beside them for their own mistakes the way beaten players do.

Johnny McGurk scored the winning point, the one that everyone remembers, but there were many vital points that day. Joe Brolly was outstanding, Brian McGilligan had a massive game in the middle of the field, and Gormley, typical Gormley, scored a few important points, including the point to take us to 0-13 each. Henry was flying and got the next and Tohill had a super game too. But a man that never got the praise he deserved for the game was Seamus Downey at full forward. He had laid off a few balls in the second half and won a couple of frees which were vital in such a close game.

But Jesus boys, we were in the All-Ireland Final and for the first time in my footballing life, I felt real pressure.

I hadn't really been too bothered in the build-up to the semi-final. Around the county the people seemed to be reserving their judgement. Too many 'nearlys' and the ageing memories of the '58 final defeat had made them a cautious people.

But after beating Dublin in their own back garden, they started to realise this team could deliver; the barriers came down, the flags went up and so did the expectations.

Letters poured in from around the country – oul' ones that remembered '58, wishing me well and saying, 'This is a good team and we'll go better than we did then', and people like myself still carrying the disappointment of 1992, great Derry people who wanted to make their feelings known and how much it meant. Having a successful county team makes you proud surely, and it means even more if you're coming for the first time.

Flags appeared on every pole in the parish and a huge Oak Leaf motif was painted at the end of our lane. But stuff like that didn't bother me, wouldn't matter to me one way or the other; that Oak Leaf was there because Derry was in an All-Ireland Final not because Eamonn Coleman lived there. That's the way I saw it and it was a good thing too; there's enough to be dealt with without building up your own ego.

But watching the Dublin game back at the lough by myself on the video, is when it really hit home. The faces in the crowd in the closing seconds of the game, the joy of the Derry people – it was unreal. It put pure pressure on me just to watch; it meant so much to them. I kept nice and cool and calm. What more could I do about it? I just had to wait for the day to come. But, it would be no good if we didn't win.

Throughout the campaign, I had been socialising as I usually did, whenever football allowed. But I was never a great man for going out of my own country much, spending whatever nights out I took at Dessie Ryan's pub in Ballyronan. Not being a drinker, there was little else to do but talk about football. It had never bothered me before but now there was no escape; ones that wouldn't have known what shape a football was wanted to talk about the team and who would be the lucky boys on the starting fifteen.

That announcement was made at the Slieve Russell hotel, the weekend before the final. The hardest team I ever had to announce because Dermot McNicholl wasn't starting – one of Derry's heroes and he was only down as a sub.

But McNicholl's reaction summed up the whole attitude in the Derry camp that year: 'Derry football is more important than Dermott McNicholl and winning the All-Ireland is the main priority.' A team man. My kind of man.

After the announcement, I headed off to Athlone for a few days, to get away from the constant phone calls, the press, to get my head cleared, just to take time. All the hard work had been done, the battle cry had been sung, now it was a matter of putting it into practice.

Arriving back at the lough that Wednesday, my heart stopped as I drove over the brow of the hill. The amount of cars sitting around the house, I thought Eliza, my aunt, had died while I was away.

People from across the country looking for tickets, refusing to believe I couldn't get them. I walked into the kitchen, into the chat and the madness that had been building across Derry and that was it, it never stopped from there.

That Wednesday evening before the final, the TV cameras was down at the lough with Michael Lyster. On the Thursday evening, myself and Mickey Moran were in Maghera with Adrian Logan. On the Friday morning, we went up to Maghera again with Joe Duffy who'd a link up with Billy Morgan back in Cork. There was a big crowd there and the remaining men of '58. South Derry had never seen the like of it; the whole thing was mighty. The phone was going constantly in the house. It was hectic.

Gary came to collect me the Saturday afternoon we were to leave for Dublin and the All-Ireland Final. As we left the house, Eliza, who was as familiar with the sports reporters of Ireland as I was myself, shouted out the door, 'Don't be coming back if you haven't got Sam Maguire'. With those words of encouragement, we were off.

On the way into Magherafelt to meet the rest of the team, we talked about nothing and everything – the hype in the county, the team Cork would field, our players and how they were holding up amongst all the attention. We never mentioned what we would do if we lost.

It was great when we got on the bus to go to Dublin. It had arrived. This was it – we only had to wait until tomorrow: destiny awaited. The send-off in Magherafelt was mighty – the crowd in the car park before we left. We were an hour getting out of the town. The emotion of it was shocking, something I hadn't been prepared for. Margaret and Vivian were there and in Moneymore, Gary's granda Teague, who had been ill, came out in the wheelchair to send him off. Once we got through Moneymore, we were able to relax and I sat back to enjoy the ride and a few games of cards with the usual squad. Pulling into the Airport Hotel in Dublin, I won the last hand; £66 was in it. Perhaps it was to be a weekend for winning.

The morning of the All-Ireland Final dawned. I was just relieved it had arrived. We were to meet at noon for a bite to eat and have a chat about the game but I was called down from my room early to sort out the first campaign of the day.

Downstairs in the hotel, the county secretary Patsy Mulholland was refusing to sign the team sheets in protest at the players not allowing Jim McGuigan on the bus to Croke Park. A protest about a protest. I hadn't time for it, hadn't the slightest inclination to be dealing with this ambush. 'He's not getting on the bus;

if he gets on the bus, the boys won't play the match.' That was that one sorted.

Arriving at Croke Park, I was the first off the bus as I needed to get the guards to form a channel for the players. In the semi-final, there was a swarm of people that they'd had to fight their way through and I wasn't going to let that happen again. Getting slapped on the back and thumped by people half drunk is not what players need and I wanted nobody to get their hands on them. When you leave the hotel on that trip to Croke Park, you just focus on the job – every minute, every man.

But when we arrived in the dressing rooms at Croke Park, I found it was my own men I should have been worrying about. We had twenty-nine players on the panel that had trained together all year. The rules state only twenty-four can tog out but in the All-Ireland hurling final the week before, Galway had twenty-one subs togged out and got fined £100 a man.

In what I saw as another example of the great team spirit within Derry that year, the players decided the extra five men would tog out too. They would all pay the fine between them, whatever that would be.

But Jesus, the hassle it created – fifteen minutes before walking out onto Croke Park and the biggest game of our lives, Patsy Mulholland and Harry Chivers, scuttling about, grabbing players by the elbow: 'Oh, we're going to be fined, we're going to be this, we're going to be that', just being a pain in the arse and annoying everyone around them.

'I've a ticket in the stand for you here, there's another one up there', they were going on, until the boys and myself had had enough of it.

One of the five, Collie McGurk, effed them out of it as they tried to bar his way onto the pitch. 'Get the fuck out of my road, the pair of yez; I've trained hard all year with the rest of them and I'm going out onto that park.'

Christ, how we ever managed to play a match, never mind an All-Ireland Final but that's what we were there for and we eventually got out to do it.

In the pre-match parade around Croke Park, Cork broke away from the Hill and the Derry supporters just as we had done with Dublin.

'Silly fuckers', I thought, 'it's dead on the first time but youse uns just look stupid.'

Perhaps they wanted to show us they meant business.

They did and in the first ten minutes of the game, scored two points and a great goal by Joe Kavanagh. Poor stuff from Derry to start.

Henry Downey had a heavy cold in the week leading up to the game and Joe Kavanagh was going past him for fun. Kavanagh's goal tore us apart but I never was one bit worried. Johnny McGurk scored the opening point to settle the boys and within seven or eight minutes, we were ahead.

Derry took over at that stage scoring 1-04, the goal coming from Seamus Downey after Niall Cahalane forced Cassidy into a cross from the corner. Downey got in between the goalkeeper and the full back to punch it into the net.

I knew we needed Enda Gormley to be at his best against this Cork team but for the first twenty minutes he never got a hand near the ball: Niall Cahalane was winning everything that came near but then Cahalane did the stupidest thing he ever could have done, hitting Gormley a dig in the back of the neck, knocking him to the ground.

The punch wakened Gormley up, angered him and the next ball that came in, he curled it over from the sideline, pointed in Cahalane's face then scored another in the next five minutes. A victim of his own stupidity, Cahalane never got a hand on Gormley in the second half. Soon after, Tony Davis got the line in the wrong, paying the price for Cahalane's dig, so changes had to be made at half time.

Taking off Damien Cassidy was a harsh substitution. He'd had a hard time against Ciaran O'Sullivan in the first ten minutes but had come well into it by the break. But we were with the extra man and I was looking to Dermott McNicholl and his surging runs and experience. McNicholl frightened players and scored a point the minute he came on.

In the heat of a game, you just never know if you're doing the right thing. You have to have the belief to trust your gut; it's a chance you have to take.

Before the game, I had wanted to play Tony Scullion on the lethal Colin Corkery but couldn't take the chance of leaving John O'Driscoll, for me that was the boy. Gary was put on Corkery but as soon as Tony Davis got the line, I moved Scullion onto Corkery who was eventually replaced that day.

O'Driscoll hadn't touched the ball but got a bit of freedom off Fergal P. McCusker. One kick and a brilliant goal – 2-08 to our 1-10.

That's the only time during the match I remember being scared. Cork had won an All-Ireland Final in 1990 with fourteen men against Meath; the referee always favours the team with fourteen, always, and I thought that Cork with fourteen men had their tails up. But we didn't panic. If that goal had been scored in 1992, we wouldn't have won the match but we had matured as a team and had learned not to change, to keep playing, not to kick the ball away – 'Just keep hold of it' was the rule.

Johnny McGurk had been playing right half-back and he became the loose man. Usually teams put the extra man up into the forward line but we kept him in at half back where he always played to let him come up the field with, and behind, the play. He scored two points in that game, a point in the first half and a point in the second half and got the Man of the Match.

It took us ten or eleven minutes before the man of the match for me – Dermot Heaney – came out to win a vital ball in the middle of the field, carrying it in and giving it to Gormley who slicked it over the bar. The equaliser.

There's always that point in a game when you know in your heart whether you'll walk away as a winner or a loser. I knew once we drew level that we were going to win the match. The next kick out, Barton got it, then Henry got it and came through before Barton was pulled down in front of the posts for a free that put us ahead. Cork never scored for the last nineteen minutes.

With five minutes to go, Gormley curled a free in from under the Hogan Stand. It was a brilliant point. It came right across and was curling out; you'd have thought it was curling wide and at the last minute, it curled in over the bar and just dropped on top of the net. That was to put us three in front and I knew Sam was going to Derry.

As a player, I'd dreamt all my life of winning the All-Ireland and now here as a manager winning it, it was the next best thing. I walked easy onto the pitch, didn't see any point in running for everyone else was scattering everywhere.

'Derry needed this All-Ireland more than Cork', said Henry Downey in his acceptance speech. I needed it more than Billy Morgan – he already had two.

But it's bullshit this about managers – players wins All-Irelands and although I was part of it, I wasn't really. Playing is the thing – nothing makes up for that. As a manager, you're in charge and you and the trainer and the selectors plan the way you play but the players is the men and that's that. Maybe it takes managers to organise, have good relationships, to know their stuff to improve the players, but managers get far too much credit and they get far too much stick.

It wasn't so much an anti-climax but I felt there should have been more. I would miss going to training, miss aiming for the goal. The dream had been realised and as soon as I achieved it, it was gone.

4 HOMECOMING HEROES

Sam had been got on 19 September 1993 and although it hadn't dawned on me as we stood in the happy madness of Croke Park, the real joy of him was still to be savoured.

We had our post-match celebration that night in the Shelbourne and the following day with the Cork team in the Burlington. We'd a Garda escort from the Airport Hotel; the outriders and all was brilliant. When we got to The Burlington, there was about 500 supporters outside and that was the start of the best part of it all.

The journey home will never be forgotten. It was really something special. People won't believe me about it not being the football but it was by far the high point for me. The sheer joy on the people's faces before we even got anywhere near our home county was brilliant. Footballers from Armagh and Tyrone, at any other time our sworn enemies, coming out on the streets in their droves to wave us on on our victory march home.

The first place we stopped in was Drogheda, then there was a bigger crowd in Dundalk. We got to the

Carrickdale Hotel at the border and I was stunned to see the huge crowd there. By the time we came out from our meal, the crowd had grown to ten times the size; it was serious. Newry was jammed as the Down people turned out in their thousands and Paddy O'Rourke, the Down captain of '91, welcomed us North with the Sam. It took us half an hour to get through Armagh or more. It was swarming with people; I'd never seen the like of it. The cup had never been as far as Armagh before – the farthest it had ever come was Newry. Donegal went the other way, by Sligo, so we were the first to bring Sam through.

At the Moy, the Tyrone men had set up a platform and Plunkett Donaghy made us a presentation. Plunkett had been unlucky enough in Derry's 1992 National League final win over Tyrone when, going up for a ball in the dying seconds of the game, it slipped through his hands and into the back of the net.

'Hey Plunkett', shouted a voice from the crowd, 'that's the second trophy you've handed to Derry.'

We were in the Moy for an hour but when we came to Cookstown, the Main Street was jammed and it took us an hour and a half to get through. By the time we'd got to the top of the town, the word had got out of our celebrations and the loyalists had cordoned it off. They wouldn't let us go down into Moneymore that way so we'd to miss out the top of the town.

I never got sick of it, not one bit – people shouting and cheering and waving at you. To come up through Tyrone with the Sam Maguire, I could have drove back up the street again just to take it in. But there was something else to it and to the Tyrone people. It wasn't just because Derry was coming through Tyrone with the Sam Maguire, it was really a show of strength by the nationalists of the county, that we're all one, you know. It was mighty. You wouldn't have believed that Tyrone and Derry hated each other so much to see the crowds waiting for us.

Then crossing the border into Derry, I saw the first bonfire outside Moneymore. Lighting the way for the returning heroes, victorious All-Ireland kings.

The players also showed their personal integrity when we'd crossed the border into the North and Jim McGuigan, who had struck their captain Downey, had been allowed on the victory bus. The county treasurer for thirty odd years, they felt, like I did, that it was the proper thing to do, so Henry and myself had went and got him off the other bus.

But even then, there was an attempt to heel us, to bring us into line by the county chairman. Harry Chivers, keen to show he was still the lynch pin. It didn't matter we'd got Sam, he was still the boss. Going to and from matches, our bus took Dungiven, Maghera, Magherafelt and Moneymore. Always. When we arrived in Moneymore, Harry wanted to take us to

Desertmartin, just deciding we weren't going through Magherafelt because that was the kind of contrary person he was. But he wasn't allowed, he didn't get his way – he was overruled by myself and the team: 'We're going through Magherafelt, the way we came and where there's a massive crowd of our supporters waiting for us.' He could dance all he wanted about being in charge, we were going where we always went. It didn't take the shine out of it one damn bit – hardly took him under my notice then but looking back after, well, you just don't know.

In those crowds through Moneymore, Magherafelt and Maghera I saw the faces of people who had been waiting the long hours for the victory bus and those of the men and women who had been waiting their whole lives. Daniel O'Donnell was in Maghera and he's a Donegal man. My family was there – something you never forget. It was the ultimate – everything you ever dreamed about all your life and you'd achieved it.

I was in Maghera all night and got back to the lough at six o'clock in the morning. Nothing was said to me for Eliza was in bed. When I get up the next day, she started talking about it and that was it; she didn't stop for about nine months.

But like any other victor, the real treat is returning in triumph to your homeland. We were heroes, one and all, and on bringing the Sam into Dessie Ryan's pub in Ballyronan the week after the All-Ireland, I saw people out on the streets that I hadn't seen in twenty odd years, out from the old people's home and from everywhere. Dungiven, Bellaghy, Derry City: the pure joy was the same. I eventually had to take myself off to the Highlands in Scotland to try and come down from the high.

But amidst the celebrations, you don't forget the men that weren't there: my da who, in his disappointment the year before, had said Sam would never come to the lough; men like Charlie Young and Jack Murphy, Ballymaguigan and football to the core and two big men in my life growing up. They were real football men who had followed Derry for years; they'd have been going to All-Irelands for years and could have mentioned the men who were playing away back in the thirties. Jack Murphy was a legend in Ballymaguigan who lived just up on the hill above us and to whose house I'd be going since I was no size – not just great Derry people but great Ballymaguigan people. All celebrations carry some sadness and so it was with the greatest celebration of them all.

But Sam Maguire was in Derry and I believed he'd be there for some time.

Anyone that's involved in football whether as players, managers or supporters doesn't follow a calendar year like normal people; the year starts when the season starts and so it has always been with me.

The year began again in October and we went well in the League up to Christmas but after that a staleness set in and we found it difficult to get back to the form we had in the lead up to the All-Ireland. But the players still had the spirit, the bond that had pushed them towards the Sam and it had showed itself again as we made to leave Maghera for our first League game against Mayo.

After the players' gesture of allowing Jim McGuigan on the team's All-Ireland homecoming bus, Jim obviously thought the row had been forgotten about. It wasn't. He was already on the coach when the players arrived in Maghera and they were refusing to get on.

'There's nothing you can do about it', I said, 'he's already on the bus but he'll not be coming into the changing rooms.' He did come into the changing rooms and Downey, amongst others, refused to tog out – in fact began getting dressed again – until I asked Jim to leave. After the game, McGuigan approached me and, with his arm across my shoulders, asked what had taken place, so I told him.

'The players were refusing to tog out unless you left the changing rooms.'

Refusing to believe it, I insisted it was the truth. He finished the conversation. 'Eamonn, I want to tell you one thing; I know what's going on back there but I know you've nothing to do with it.' He was right but it meant little to me. As long as it didn't affect the team, I didn't give a damn.

We moved on in the National League, picking up some injuries, but it had taken so much to win the All-Ireland, we had achieved what we wanted to achieve and in the months of February and March, it was hard to get the hunger up again.

We went out of the National League to Westmeath at the quarter-final stages. A lot of people were disappointed but myself or the players weren't too heartbroken. We had trained long and hard in '93 and getting into a League semi-final would have been a bit much after all the training.

We didn't go out to get beaten. Derry never went out to get beaten but the rumour mill was spinning and before long it was round the county that players, and maybe even myself included, had placed bets on a Westmeath win. Pure nonsense, pure crap. That was a game to bet on if you were a betting person but I'd never heard such bullshit in my life. Rumours and half-truths abound in the GAA world; it bugs you at the time but all in all it's like water off a duck's back.

What it did mean though was that the defeat gave heart to the other teams; after all, if Westmeath could beat us, Down could beat us and that's how it turned out.

The 1977 All-Ireland Semi-Final between Dublin and Kerry had long been regarded as the best football

Derry players training at St Trea's, Ballymaguigan, in the run-up to the final.

The Derry squad of 1993 at Croke Park on All-Ireland Final day. Photographer Danny O'Kane recalled Eamonn's meticulous preparations in the week before the game, calling him to a training session to practice the photo being taken. 'He wanted the players to know exactly where they should stand on the day, so they would be calm and prepared and have a focus.'

Expectant Derry fans on Hill 16.

The starting fifteen: Back row, left to right: Joe Brolly, Dermot Heaney, Anthony Tohill, Damien McCusker, Seamus Downey, Tony Scullion, Damien Barton and Brian McGilligan.

Front row, left to right: Enda Gormley, Johnny McGurk, Henry Downey, Kieran McKeever, Gary Coleman, Fergal P. McCusker and Damien Cassidy.

Eamonn surveys the scene ahead of the final with Croke Park officials. RTÉ presenter Marty Morrissey can be seen in the background.

Joe Brolly shrugs off the attentions of Cork's Brian Corcoran in the All-Ireland Final on 19 September 1993.

Anthony Tohill beats Cork's Steven O'Brien to an aerial ball.

Tony Scullion steadies his manager as delirious fans attempt to reach him on the steps at Croke Park.

One of those who manages to get through is Donegal manager Brian McEniff, showing his delight at his old foe's All-Ireland triumph.

Gary Coleman is congratulated on the Croke Park steps by teammate Eugene Kelly.

Ulster GAA President Peter Quinn hands over the Sam Maguire to Henry Downey with the then Taoiseach Albert Reynolds looking on.

Triumphant captain Henry Downey raises the Sam Maguire cup for the first time in Derry's history. (Image courtesy of Sportsfile.)

A jubilant Eamonn holds the Sam Maguire aloft, the only Derry manager ever to do so.

Dungiven welcomes back Derry's All-Ireland kings on the Tuesday after the victory, just one of a series of uproarious celebrations across the county that week.

Awards and accolades also followed for Eamonn. Here, he is presented with a Coach of the Year award by his footballing hero and fellow Ballymaguigan man, Jim McKeever.

Eamonn with the seven Derry players named All Stars for 1993. Back row, left to right: Anthony Tohill, Enda Gormley, Tony Scullion and Brian McGilligan. Front row, left to right: Johnny McGurk, Eamonn, Footballer of the Year Henry Downey and Gary Coleman.

match ever to be played in Ireland. The semi-final of Derry and Dublin in '93 would rate very high and also the Derry v Down game in Casement in '92 but for me, Derry and Down at Celtic Park in the first round of the '94 Ulster championship was the best match ever played. There were less fouls, less wide balls, great passing, and sportsmanship – an outstanding game of football.

We had beaten Down in that great game of football in Casement Park in 1992 and had annihilated them in the Marshes in '93. I believe to this day that their humiliation following that defeat spurred them on to the victory of '94.

The injuries we had suffered also dealt us a heavy blow. Johnny McGurk, Tony Scullion and Damien Barton were all hurt. Gary was still struggling with fitness after getting thirty-eight stitches in his leg after a League game against Kildare at Ballinascreen. Enda Gormley had been struggling with fitness too.

But I still believed we'd the beating of them and after Down scored the first point, Derry went into a 04-01 lead. Anthony Tohill broke through and the goalkeeper made a tremendous save and I think if that had gone into the net, the game would've been over.

Mickey Linden was flying and scored five points off Gary in the first half. Down had moved James McCartan out of the full forward line to get him away from Kieran McKeever. McKeever had to be moved onto Linden but he'd the damage done by then. Johnny McGurk wasn't fit to play, otherwise he'd have picked up McCartan who was also flying in the half back line. A Catch 22 situation. Scullion carrying a hamstring injury at full back, Gary not match fit at left full back and Henry taking a roasting from Greg Blayney – no, things weren't going well. But I still felt we had the winning of the match and two points behind at half time seemed nothing in a match like this.

It was Fergal P. who gave us the jump we needed with a goal fifteen minutes into the second half. Immediately after, Tohill kicked a wide with Declan Bateson through for a goal inside. If he had even taken a point, Down were gone at that stage but they got off the hook. Like Down in '92 and Donegal in '93, our hunger was gone; the real appetite wasn't back. But that was some Down team and a great Derry team – the two best teams in the country at that stage playing a great game of football but with us on the losing end of it. Never mind the 'classic' tag, I would have settled for a terrible game of football and a Derry win. Never worry how you go down; you go down, you're beat and that's it.

We were disappointed but it was nothing like the defeat against Donegal in '92. We had our National League title in 1992, our All-Ireland of 1993. We had the players, a young team and we would be back, rested and recharged to win the All-Ireland of 1995. It was just football. Every team that won an All-Ireland at that time got beat the following year: it happened to Down in '91, it happened to Donegal in '92 and it happened to Derry in '93. The team was there and they knew how to win but it was just one of those days. A few injuries, players under par but they hadn't become bad players overnight – perhaps I had become a bad manager overnight. After all, managers don't win matches – managers just loses them.

But even in defeat, we were a real band having trained steadily together for two years.

On the coach home, talk turned to the long summer without football, how we would miss the training and how would you put the nights in. When there's no football, what do you do? Tohill said he might head to America. 'Why don't you come too?' he said. That was the first I heard of America and at that stage, I'd no intentions of going.

Every place I'd went to around home that week, the people was talking about the match and I just had to face up to it. We were out and we had to wait another year, or that's what I thought.

Later that week, I got a call from Chicago and decided then I might as well go to St Brendan's in Chicago where Tohill was going, to coach and manage the team. I didn't tell the county board I was going. The football was finished in Derry and I'd be back before the training started in September but I had things to sort out with my selectors and management team.

There was a question at that time that Mickey Moran, who had been such a tremendous coach, wasn't going to stay another year. Myself, Mickey, Harry Gribben and Dinny McKeever met at Dinny's house, just above my own in Ballymaguigan, to discuss it.

'Eamonn, I was going to step down but if you're going to stay another year, I'll stay too', were Mickey's words to me that evening.

I had intended on giving it one more year anyway. So, we agreed between us that while I was away, Harry Gribben and Mickey Moran would go to the Derry championship to see was there any players in Derry other than those we'd got on the panel. 'What's in Derry we have on the panel', added Mickey which all of us knew was true. Whatever, though, I'd be back before the All-Ireland Final.

'If there's any problems comes up, I'll phone you in America', said my selector Harry Gribben, and that's the last civil conversation I had with him.

5 BACK-ROOM BETRAYAL

There is an image of me in the GAA world, and even in the smaller circles around me, as a tough, distrusting, money man; a manipulator of the media and my opponents, a closed and secretive individual whose own family have been known to say: 'He'd hardly tell himself what he was doing, in case he found out about it himself.'

It wasn't always so and in large part, it isn't true but in 1994, I learnt the hardest lessons of my life and swore then that I would never fall to the same mistakes again.

I had had a brilliant time in Chicago: me, Tohill, Kieran McKeever, Enda Gormley and Gary, who'd all gone out to St Brendan's, being allowed to transfer for the summer. The American championship wasn't knockout like Ulster, so other men would come out to America as they become available. There were home-based teams but all the big stars were from Ireland, and there was a lot of Southern men there too, living close to each other, playing football and having the craic. After the disappointment of the Down game, for me it was a relief.

Eamonn Burns came out to join us around July and mentioned to Tohill the rumblings he'd heard in Derry about moves to get me out.

Naïve? Jesus when I think about it now … We laughed, took it as a joke and carried on. It never even entered my head a second time.

The Tuesday before I was due home, the county chairman Harry Chivers rang me in Chicago to ask was I letting my name go forward for selection for another year as the Derry manager. I said I was.

It was Thursday evening when he called me again and these were his exact words: 'I always get the dirty jobs to do.' It never fizzed on me for a second. 'I have to tell you Eamonn, you didn't get the Derry job.'

Still nothing – it was like auto pilot.

'Who got it?'

'I'm not allowed to say.'

'Ok.' That was it.

Standing in an apartment in Chicago, thousands of miles from home. It couldn't be right. Five minutes passed, ten minutes. The bastards … the dirty bastards. What is this?

Anger set in and I lifted the phone. I still hadn't fully clicked on but knew I had to do something. Were they trying to get rid of me just like that? Is that it? Is that me done? I called a friend at home. I had to let people know what was happening.

'Phone RTÉ's Brian Carthy in Dublin and tell him what has happened. They're not going to sweep this under the carpet.' So, the news was on the airwaves in Ireland before anyone in Derry had been told – before Gary knew, before any of my family knew.

Arriving at Dublin airport on the Sunday morning, Liam Hayes, the former Meath player and a friend of mine at the time, picked me up from the airport.

'Did you hear who got the Derry job?'

'Nobody's got it', I said, still stupid about what was going on.

'Mickey Moran was appointed at quarter past eleven last night.'

I was gutted. Stunned. What is this? What's going on here? Mickey, who I'd worked with for four years and who I would have trusted with my life. Mickey, who the year before the All-Ireland had threatened to resign after a row with the county secretary Patsy Mulholland. Patsy Mulholland had jacked the job in for about three months and Mickey was going to resign too. Mickey who was persuaded to stay after I told the county chairman Harry Chivers, 'If he goes, I go.' I had stood by him. He didn't stand by me.

It was hard to take in and it was hurtful to take in but bits of the jigsaw finally started to drop into place. I'd been betrayed. It was that simple. I was still convinced there was no way the county board could justify sacking me. I'd done nothing wrong. But it was obvious there had been plenty of work going on behind backs and my men, who I'd backed to the hilt, had deserted me for they were still in and I was gone.

If there were any problems, my men were going to phone me. I challenged Harry Gribben. He'd lost my phone number. Jim McGuigan knew 'what was going on back there' but knew 'it had nothing to do with me'. He couldn't remember saying that. Mickey had sat and told me he would only stay on as coach if I stayed on as manager. The players challenged him at a meeting two weeks later in Toome. He was just 'keeping the thing going until we get Eamonn reinstated'. They gave him a fortnight to speak to the county board but when Henry Downey went back to see him, he admitted he wanted the job.

There was nobody wanted the job in 1991 but there was plenty wanted it in 1994. They knew the team was there to win another All-Ireland and they were looking to do it without me.

I might have been the only Derry manager to have won an All-Ireland but for me it was all about the players. It was always about the players and me backing them with McGuigan had just proved it. It actually didn't bother me either way who was right or wrong in the matter but as a manager, sticking by the players was my job; that's who I was there to look after and anybody who says any different is a fool.

I was got rid of because player power was raising its ugly head in Derry again and the county board men, who felt the success of Derry should anchor around them and not the players, were prepared to axe me, happy to axe me, to make sure the uprising was trampled.

I remembered back to 1990 and my first meeting with the county board after being approached to take the Derry job. The issue of player power had been raised that night. In the late 1980s, Tom Scullion, Phil Stewart and one of my footballing heroes, Jim McKeever, had formed the management team of a Derry side beaten in the semi-final of the 1987 All-Ireland. After that defeat, the three had resigned. However, it was widely accepted that the grumblings of the players in the dressing rooms had removed them from their posts.

'We let those boys down', said one of those men the evening I took the job. 'There'll never be player power in Derry again', he pledged.

They saw me as adding weight to the power the players had begun to exercise in not letting McGuigan onto the bus, in standing by their captain. It was their own mistake. If the board had dealt with the McGuigan mess, the players wouldn't have needed to flex any muscle whatsoever. But I was never a favourite with the county board anyway having spoken openly in the press about the financial sacrifices made by myself and other GAA managers.

At one stage, I'd been pulled aside by my selector Harry Gribben, in Spain, where we had gone after winning the All-Ireland. Harry, in his wisdom, had warned me off being friends with and getting too great with the players. After ten years as a manager and a successful one at that, I thought it was a load of bullshit and jealousy.

I had nothing in common at all with the men who filled the boards and councils. Since boyhood, being a football player was all that filled my life. When that finished, managing players was the next best thing. For me football was all about a green field, nothing to do with jumped up little nothings, full of their own self-importance in committee rooms across the country.

The players refused to train under Mickey Moran and at the start of the National League, refused to tog out. There was to be a training session on the Thursday night.

Not having training to be at, I was in Dessie Ryan's pub in Ballyronan and a man named Patsy Forbes came to see me. A Tyrone man living in Magherafelt, he was a big GAA man and would have done a lot of fundraising for Derry. He said there was a meeting in Toome and then there was to be training at Greenlough but there was rumblings that the players weren't going to train. 'We'll have to sort this out', he said. 'Will you meet Mickey Moran this evening?'

My words to Patsy was, 'I'll meet him at anytime as I have nothing to hide', and I never heard another word about it.

The loss of the one job that meant everything in the world to me was bad enough to take but it went deeper than that, far deeper, and yes, deeper even than football. When, five weeks after my sacking, the county board eventually agreed to meet me, the four reasons given by the board members present were laughable, never mind pathetic.

They spoke about my giving a few nights to the Kildress club in training; speaking in public about my expenses from the board; trying to make money from a committee outside the county board and taking players to America.

My first move into management had been with the Tyrone club Kildress and I'd been asked to give them a hand training during 1994 – a few nights here or there. I'd been happy to do it.

The second of their reasons related to a question and answer session I had taken part in in Donegal when I had been asked was it true that I received £200 a week expenses from the Derry county board. Laughing, I had replied, not at all. I got £50 expenses and that was it.

The third was my approaching the supporters club in September of 1993 when I asked would they be willing to compensate me for loss of wages for the week before and after the All-Ireland Final. I had already asked the county board for an additional £50 for each of those two weeks and they had refused. The move was more to embarrass the county board into at least acknowledging the fact that it was impossible for me to work at that time but I was expected to bear the loss of income. They must have dug deep to come up with that one, I thought.

As for the American crap, to even utter that I had deliberately lost a match, given up another shot at an All-Ireland for Derry, let Sam go to Down just to get to America – bullshit all of it and they knew it.

If I had failed as a manager then sack me for failing as a manager. I'm a big boy; I could've handled that. But after forty-seven games in charge, forty-two wins, a National League title and the county's first ever All-Ireland, they couldn't say that.

What I can never forgive though is the spineless way they went about it in their eagerness to take Derry's glory. What they did was to leave a cloud of suspicion hanging over me and through that, over my family.

The rumours were thick, not only in Derry but across the country. People that wouldn't know me were thinking, 'He must have done something terrible', 'There's no smoke without fire'. Time and again I called on the county board to make public the charges against me, to lay it on the line why they sacked me and they never did. They refused because there were none and the only way they could disguise their actions was to direct the attention towards me. There was nothing else they could do. They knew, and more importantly the players knew, I had done nothing wrong. That's why the players were so staunch behind me.

But the board underestimated the team, and the bond between them and me. They didn't realise how close we were. I was like one of them; we would have talked about anything, craiced about anything, oul' chat and bad chat about what they'd been up to. They thought they could step right into that but instead they shattered it and the whole thing fell apart.

Before that meeting at a hotel in Claudy, the players were still refusing to train, so Brian McGilligan, Henry Downey and Kieran McKeever went to meet the county board about half an hour before I was due in. They wanted me reinstated but the county board got their way.

I knew it was over. I knew what had been done so I held a meeting with the players in Ballymaguigan. Time had gone on, meetings followed meetings, there'd been protests by the players and bad craic in the press but those jumped up little nothings had got their way and I was really done as Derry's manager.

I told them to go back, said Derry was bigger than Mickey Moran or myself or anybody and if it was me, I'd go back and play. They didn't want to budge and some were more vocal than others. Damien McCusker,

Enda Gormley, Fergal P., Gary, Johnny McGurk, Henry Downey, Jonathon Kelly, Damien Cassidy, Dermot McNicholl, no players wanted to go back.

It was a long, emotional meeting and it took it out of the lot of us but they finally decided, one goes back or nobody goes back. They were still that team. Enda Gormley and Damian McCusker were adamant they wouldn't do it but Brian McGilligan said he agreed with me and they should all go back together. I remember then Gormley, getting all reared up asking, 'I wonder Brian, will we all be together again as Champions in the heat of Clones?' They never were.

They knew what the county board had done was just spiteful. They realised that the amount of work that we had all put into it, but myself in particular, had been thrown away and what was left was a spent force. Henry Downey had said in his All-Ireland victory speech that I was Derry football itself. The county board was envious that the players thought of me like that and they were going to put a spanner in the works whatever happened and my back-up team fell for it.

Those people who see me as distrustful and suspicious are those that know nothing about me. Every player on that panel trusted me as I trusted them, as I did my management team, to my cost. The county board's dealings left the Derry team with a legacy of mistrust and ruined its chances of, if not two, at least one more All-Ireland.

Whether the supporters realised that or not – and I believe the genuine fans did – the people of Derry didn't have long to wait to get their answer. In the Ulster Semi-Final of 1995 Tyrone beat that great young team with thirteen men in Clones – Tyrone, who had come from nowhere and went on to get beaten by Dublin in a bad game of football in the All-Ireland Final. The county board's actions were clearly shown up that day in Clones.

The team was split and never regrouped, never came together again. That's the damage they did. There was the National League titles of '95 and '96 but no Ulster championships and no All-Irelands.

It wasn't that Mickey Moran was a bad manager, as he has proved with Sligo and Donegal, but he hadn't got the backing of the players. To win an Ulster championship, an All-Ireland, everybody needs to be pulling the same way, 100 per cent, but the whole thing was shattered and by the end of it all, so was I. People that I trusted let me down and that affected me as a person.

I've always been one who would keep a lot of things to himself; if you don't tell people then things won't be told. But I was never cynical enough to even think about harmless day-to-day events being used against me. Training Kildress? How could I have known that would be used as a stick to beat me with? I'll know the next time, I thought.

As a man that wouldn't let too many people close to me, what friends I have would be good friends. I viewed those men as such. Mickey Moran, Harry Gribben and Dinny McKeever were my friends and we worked alongside each other. I took it for granted, never even doubted that they would work to the same ideas of friendship as my own. Trust, respect and loyalty? I felt a damned fool.

The men in the committee rooms who thought I put too much by the players – the Harry Chivers, Bernie Mullans, Willie Turners, Patsy Mulhollands – they had got their way and my men, my back-up team, had fell in with them as part of it. They wanted the glory? They could have it. I didn't have the stomach for it anymore.

6 NO MAGIC IN MANAGEMENT

A lways the boy for making a lasting impression, I broke the ankle of my first county manager when I was just seventeen.

Fr Seamus Shields was manager of the 1965 All-Ireland-winning minor team and for me, he was the man who set Derry football on its way. A small man with black wavy-hair and a dynamic, powerful individual, he was somebody you could respect and me and him would have had a brilliant, brilliant relationship.

He'd have stood along the line in his collar and black coat, but this day, he got in my way, being too far on the pitch. Playing Antrim at Casement Park, I went out for the ball and drove into him after an Antrim fella crashed into me. He had to be carried off the pitch and away off to the hospital and he always said he never would forgive me 'til we won the All-Ireland At the hotel in Malahide, the night we minors celebrated that All-Ireland win, he touched on it in his speech and said he had forgiven me because we had achieved what we'd set out to do.

Driven and determined, with a real glint in his eye when he spoke, he had started the Co-Op in Swatragh, bringing business into the area. Bringing that force and those organisational skills when he came to take on the minors, he introduced the structures that were badly missing in the county set up.

There had been quite a number of good teams in Derry, as the team that reached the All-Ireland Final against Dublin in '58 had proved, but the structure of it was missing and all it came down to was a bit of organising.

In the early sixties, like for most other families in the country, there was no car at our house, so I'd no way of going to training if it wasn't in my home parish. One evening after work, I was heading out our road when I met a taxi coming down and asked him who he was looking for. He'd been told to collect me and I'd to get back and get my kit. The taxi was collecting the minors to take them to training. I never dreamt of a taxi coming for me in my life. I thought I was great. But that was the rock on which everything was built – Fr Shields sending taxis. When you're winning, people gives you all these names and when you're getting beat you're useless, but you can't manage a team if there's nobody there to manage.

The Derry minor team had never fared too well in the Ulster minor championship but Fr Shields came in the early sixties and by 1965, we were All-Ireland minor champions. He had brought Derry through;

the county had got its first ever All-Ireland title and a couple of years after that, Fr Shields was out.

I was a young player and too caught up in what was happening. I didn't know much of what was going on when he just disappeared off the scene. I was coming on to the senior team and I'd have been leaving that behind, but he never featured after that.

He wouldn't have known a lot about football tactically but he'd a great driving force in him, a great spirit and was good with people. You need to be a psychologist to be a good manager; it's definitely more than 50/50. If you're friendly and the better you get on with people, the more you get out of them. But he knew enough to bring in Sean O'Connell as trainer, who I would rate very highly in knowing about football.

Sean O'Connell from Ballerin trained that minor team with Fr Shields and at underage level, was another massive influence for me. From being my first trainer at county level, he played up until 1976 and me and him played together in an Ulster Railway Cup as well as in the Ulster Final of 1970 against Antrim. He played at right half forward and was a great free taker as well as a great score taker from play – two footed and very quick. A brilliant footballer and the leading scorer in Derry for years, in Ulster and in Ireland, he was nineteen in 1958 when he scored the goal that took Derry to their first senior All-Ireland Final.

Sean had a great understanding of the game and he got on very well with the players. He never, ever panicked and always seemed to know exactly what to say and what to do. Coming out in the All-Ireland minor final against Kerry, I had kicked two wides and he said, 'The next ball you get now, Eamonn, don't kick it, carry it.' Then I scored the next three points in a row.

I'd been doing alright through the minor campaign and had got a goal in the Ulster Final where we beat Cavan by ten points, 3-11 to 2-04. In the semi-final against Roscommon, we were seven points down at one stage and I got the goal that put us into the final. Scoring the goal to get your team to the final was great. Aw, I felt brilliant, but to get playing in Croke Park, there at the other end of the world, was the big thing for us. And to win an All-Ireland away there in Dublin …

Sean O'Connell took the team after Fr Shields and managed us as U21s when we went on to win the All-Ireland in 1968. When I played minor football and at U21, I never had dreamt about being a manager, but I suppose you have these influences, all these great men throughout your life. I'd looked up to Sean as a player but the man, the leader who I looked up to most; he was a Ballymaguigan man living across the fields from me.

'Gentleman', Jim McKeever was the big name throughout Ireland, captain of the 1958 All-Ireland finalists and the local hero in my townland. It was him brought me into the senior team when I was just fourteen although he wasn't managing, he was playing.

I was down watching Ballymaguigan train for the senior championship ahead of the semi-final when Jim McKeever asked me to train with them. I used to go along at that time with my pack: the arms of the jersey stretched and tied up and the boots and the pants inside it. I never dreamed about playing, just thought they'd asked me to train with them because I was there.

John McGlone and John McCartney were two working men from the townland who had been looking after the team around 1962 but for me, Jim McKeever was the man. As well as being a legend in Derry, people throughout Ireland was inspired by him so you can imagine what somebody of fourteen felt when the likes of him even bothered to talk to him.

In the county final of 1962 that we played against Castledawson, I was good enough to be on the team, but he wouldn't let them start me I was that young. The first match was a drawn game, so I came on at half-time in the final, scored a goal and a point and was carried off the field a real hero, the youngest ever player to win a senior county medal. You don't think about these things at the time but, having been part of the team to win Ballymaguigan's first ever senior county championship, I thought about that surely.

McKeever would have been a hero of mine, no doubt, no matter where he would have come from but that connection with Ballymaguigan is something very special. Country people, even if they don't get on at all, is really, really close when they get on a football field. There's great craic when everyone's heart's in it. It's my community, our community; I've always felt like that.

I had played my schoolboy football for Ballinderry and had left Ballymaguigan to go and play for them in 1975 and it was the worst thing I ever did, despite winning a senior championship with them in 1981. It had nothing to do with Ballinderry. They were a good team and good fellas and still are, but you just want the boys that you ran about with – like, Ballinderry's Adrian McGuckin, who I'd played with through the minors and on; him and myself was very close and still are. But they weren't the boys you went to dances with and went to school with. I enjoyed it there, but I never enjoyed it as much as when I was playing for Ballymaguigan, playing for my own parish.

When Gary came out from Magherafelt to live here at the lough, I encouraged him to join the team. Football in Magherafelt is not the same as in Ballymaguigan. If you're not a townie, they won't accept you; you're still an outsider and that'd be the same in parishes across the country. If you're living in a place and you want to borrow a tractor or anything, you don't go to Magherafelt to look for it. Those connections, both near you and across the county, needs to stick to win All-Irelands.

To win an All-Ireland takes lots of things and lots of luck but you need to have a good management team that gets on well together. You need commitment and belief and to let the players know you really believe in them and that you're going to be fair. But no individual can win a team an All-Ireland he's only part of the arm, he's only a finger on the hand that's achieved that.

I try to have them all as a big happy family playing for each other. Sometimes it works and sometimes it doesn't; it depends on the players. The players that's playing on the team always thinks more of the manager than the boys that's not but if players feel that you know what you're doing, you're halfway there. Nobody knows quicker than players if a manager or a trainer doesn't know what he's at but if the players feel that the management team knows exactly where they're going, it helps the team in a big way.

Sean O'Connell was a brilliant player and a brilliant manager and so was Jim McKeever, but I don't believe that you can only truly understand football or be a great manager if you've played it yourself. What you do have to have been is a thinking player. There's those that never played but they're thinkers – those that knows the game.

But the most success in building a team is you need to be fit to work with people, all people. I would have talked to the players and discussed things with them; it wasn't like I was laying down the law. We had the players and we had a very good management team, I thought, and everybody seemed to know what was happening. Mickey Moran, Dinny McKeever and Harry Gribben always got on fine as far as I was concerned.

But the mindset, the psychology is crucial and at the start of '93, we brought in some help. Professor Craig Mahoney, who was originally from Australia, was a sports psychologist who'd been working at Queen's University in Belfast. Craig planned the fitness programme with the help of Mickey Moran and myself and other than that, he would talk to an odd individual. He said very little but when he did speak, he was effective.

After Donegal had beat us in the National League quarter-final in '93, on that Easter Sunday in Breffni Park, we'd had a meeting the following Monday night in Ballymaguigan. It lasted four hours and there was a lot of spades called a spade that night, but many people believe it was the meeting that won Derry the All-Ireland.

At that meeting, Craig was excellent. We had played well in the first half and then had fell away and although we knew it was fitness, we were still worried because we were beaten. We wanted to leave nothing to chance going into the Down game four weeks later so everybody was at it, the players, and the management.

During the Donegal match, Dermot McNicholl had come to the sideline for a drink of water and Craig asked him why he had come at that stage. A free had been missed by Gormley and he asked him, 'Why did you miss the free?' We looked at absolutely everything; it was a vital meeting.

The difference between success and failure is very slim, that bit between winning and losing. Like, just because you're beaten in an All-Ireland Final doesn't mean you're not as good as the team that won; the only difference would be that a ball that somebody kicked would hit the post and come back out and one at the other end went over. But that'll never be remembered.

In 2000, Kerry drew against Armagh in an All-Ireland Semi-Final and Kerry won the replay by a goal. I always feel Armagh was a better team that day and should have won the match. Oisin McConville kicked the ball up against the goalkeeper in the dying seconds and that was the difference that day. It didn't mean Kerry was the better team. Success is what you're remembered by, but it's not always the story.

The story in Ulster in the early nineties was one of success though. I hadn't believed the rest of the country was going down; it was just that Ulster had got very strong. That had gone back maybe six or eight years before, starting the process right through from the schools. Ulster football had taken over at schools level: Adrian McGuckin had won two Hogan Cups with Maghera when Anthony Tohill, Eamonn Burns and them fellas came through and Ray Morgan and Pete McGrath had done it in Down with St Colman's in Newry.

Donegal had won an U21 All-Ireland in 1987 after a replay with Kerry, then the universities had taken over. Jordanstown and Queen's had been big forces in college football and started winning Sigersons in the eighties and St Mary's had got one as well. That really brought football on, especially in Down and Derry.

Jordanstown's two Sigerson Cup teams in '85 and '86, that I was in charge of along with Charlie Sweeney, had D.J. Kane and Barry Breen of Down that went on to win All-Ireland medals. Then you had Enda Gormley and Dermott McNicholl on the Derry team, so the flow of players had been coming through the three counties. They were coming though from minors, U21s and colleges which saw Ulster football really take off.

The two big men then in Ulster were: McGrath and McEniff. You had to be looking at what they did but you also took on board the Sean Boylans, the Kevin Heffernans, the Mick O'Dwyers, the men who had done it so often, but because McEniff and McGrath were beside me in Ulster, you had to look closely at them. Down had won it, Donegal had won it and Derry were coming looking for it.

They had got success, so you had to look at how they'd got it. And they got it the way we did: a good management team putting a good team of players together, plenty of hard work and plenty of long nights.

Pete McGrath would be a very quiet man and other than speaking to him after a match, him and myself would never, ever have had words. McEniff and myself, on the other hand, would have had words loads of times, not that we'd be any worse friends at the end of the day.

Pete McGrath was a gentleman, a real gentleman and proved he was a great manager, winning two All-Irelands, one in '91 and one in '94. Any manager that wins two All-Ireland in the space of three years, it speaks for itself and, I have to say, he won them with some limited footballers. He had some great players too but he really got the best out of the lesser boys.

He got himself into a bit of bother after we'd beat them in 1993 and the Massacre at the Marshes. The players didn't like it because they felt he was putting the defeat on them. But the following year, he turned that round and them players beat Derry in Derry city in probably the best game of football ever played. Everybody does things wrong at times and even if Pete said things he shouldn't have, he certainly put it right twelve months later.

My own way of going on is, if you're going to criticise players, you do it in the privacy of the dressing room. I would criticise referees in public but if I've something to say to a player, I'll do it in private and to their face and not through the press or anyone else. The press criticise players enough and very little do they know about it.

Brian McEniff took a team from nowhere and won an All-Ireland and three Ulster titles, the first in 1983. He introduced a new style of play to Donegal; they didn't kick the ball away – a style we preached too in those early years. Donegal was a small team, small players, and it was harder for them to get possession of the ball so when they got it they tried not to give it away.

I had played in the Ulster Railway Cup team back in the seventies with McEniff but I wouldn't have known too much about him. He was good at his business and he was good at football management; he had the success to prove it.

He'd have been quieter than me, I'd say. I might shout at some player but I don't continually rant and roar, not at all, there's no point. People see me jumping up and down but that's just yourself, you know. If somebody makes a mistake, you can see it. And it's exhausting, the most exhausting thing, a big game like an All-Ireland Semi-Final or an Ulster Final. In big games like that, it's worse than playing

… mentally you'd be exhausted. I think so anyway. When you're on the pitch playing, really, you're just playing your position and trying to do your best in that area. When you manage a team, you're looking all over the field, trying so suss out what's happening, trying to improve what's going on. I would try and see a weakness in the opposition and punish it and the emotion of it, it's terrible. You feel like sleeping after the match is over – well, it's like that with the Championship, National League matches. I can't speak for other managers but I'd say it takes it out of everybody.

But, definitely the most important thing is the way you feel and the way the players feel. If you feel in yourself that you're good enough to do the job, then there's never the same pressure on you. I always felt I was good enough to do it, so you can call that big headed or whatever you like but it gives you confidence that you know what you're doing. And I always felt, from when I started to get involved with people, that I got on well. I was straight with them and I always got the best out of them. If you don't have an overall confidence in yourself then you shouldn't take the job.

You might say myself, Pete McGrath and McEniff just happened to be in the right place at the right time with the results of all that hard work coming through the structures and the counties. I believe we were the right men in the right place to channel the right talent at the right time.

But the work it takes is tarra. Managing a county team is like managing a team in the English Premiere League, only you've to go to work as well: you're involved in training at least three nights of the week and at a meeting another night, you're on the phone steady, you're arranging challenge matches and talking about football to whoever you meet. You do it all for the love of the game but my love of the game's run out. I'm tired now, well tired and I'll be glad to give it up. I retired before and I was genuine then, surely. I stayed away six weeks. But I think I'll be glad to leave it behind because it doesn't come as easy to me now. I would be soft really and it's harder to bollock somebody now than it was in '92 or '93. I'm more mature, mellowed by time and when you mellow you lose something, you know. And I'm giving it up because I've put enough time into it. Simple as that.

I have always maintained you never celebrate enough when you win the way you grieve when you lose and if we had lost the All-Ireland it would have bugged me for all my life. It's tarra; a team like that, that only won one All-Ireland – '95 and '96 could have been theirs. Them was vital years. They were gone in '97, the day Cavan beat them in the Ulster Final. They were on the back foot.

But nobody can take it away from us. The boys of '93 is still the men – the only Derry men to ever win the All-Ireland. They're the best Derry players that ever was. They're the best Derry players that ever was because they have All-Ireland medals to prove it.

FAMILY MATTERS
by Gary Coleman

'*Of course they were targeting him; that was the idea of it, to get at me. I knew it was going on but there was nothing I could do about it. The county board was rubbing it in. But it all came back to haunt them in '95 when Tyrone beat them: the Three Wise Men standing along the line. A Tyrone team that came from nowhere against a team that had won three National League titles and had been All-Ireland champions. This young Tyrone team came along, beat them in '95 and took a hand out of them completely in '96.*'

Eamonn Coleman, April 2002

'*The night Daddy died on 11 June 2007, I took a phone call from Mickey Moran. It can't have been easy for him to do as we hadn't spoken in ten years or more and he'd have had no idea of the reception he would get. He passed on his sympathies but said he couldn't make the wake as he was going on holidays in the early hours of the next morning. The following week he called to my house, we embraced, we got emotional and we talked.*

After a while, I took him to Daddy's grave where we stood side by side. This is an account of my experience of the mid-nineties, but I appreciated – and still do – Mickey's actions of 2007.'

Gary Coleman, June 2018

The first I knew of Daddy being sacked was coming out of work in Magherafelt on the Saturday he was due home from America. I met a boy in the car park, Philip McKeown, a county board member from South Derry; we sat in the car and he told me.

I'd heard the rumblings that Eamonn Burns was talking about when he'd come out to join us in Chicago. But like everybody else I thought it was nonsense. How could it be anything else? It hadn't been made public then and I hadn't been talking to him; he was on his way back from the States. But I was shocked – I couldn't believe it – shocked and cross too.

I'd to pick him up from Dundalk and, struggling with it myself, asked him what he was going to do. It was hard to know what he was like at that stage. He was cross, I knew that much. He just said, 'What could he do?' He was going to find out why and he wanted to wait and see what was happening.

Mickey Moran had been on the radio on the Saturday night to say that if the players didn't want him to take the job he wouldn't. But on the Sunday around 1 pm it was announced on the sports news that he'd been appointed as manager. I was raging, absolutely raging. I knew then he had stabbed him in the back.

I didn't know what to do so I went to Dinny McKeever, a friend of our family for manys a year. When I got to the house, Harry Gribben's car was sitting outside but I gave him the benefit of the doubt. When I called back, I asked Dinny what he was going to do and he told me he hadn't thought about it. I warned him of the rumblings and that the players weren't happy and if he was wise he wouldn't go near it. The next thing I heard, the whole management team was back in so I knew Dinny had done the dirt on him too.

The players were disgusted, I was disgusted and we weren't going to let it go. The following week I was talking to a player who said he'd see me at the meeting on Tuesday. I hadn't even heard about it. On the Tuesday morning I got a letter through the post from Harry Gribben which read, 'Gary there will be a meeting of players in Toome hotel, Tuesday, eight o'clock. I lost your phone number, Harry.'

After Mickey Moran spoke that evening, I stood up and asked about the call. I was the only one to get a letter. Harry Gribben said it was his fault because he had lost my phone number. 'Thirty-two people in this room, Harry', I said, 'and the only number you lost was Eamonn Coleman's son's. You're nothing but a cowardly cunt.' The atmosphere was tarra. There was pure rage from the boys; the management team were shaking. Mickey Moran had his speech all wrote out but had to sit the paper he was holding on the table, he and it were shaking that much.

'He wasn't to blame for taking on the job.' He said, Daddy had 'gone to America and lied to him'. He started blaming Daddy. He said he'd told him he wouldn't be taking on any teams so when he heard about St Brendan's he felt betrayed so he was going to take the job. Now what that had to do with it I don't know and if it was the best he could come up with it was poor. The players were so disgusted he backed down and said if we didn't want him he'd step down.

Because Daddy's sacking had been such a shock, there had been a whole lot already said in the press and Mickey said nothing should leave the room. I'd had a tape recorder in my pocket but the thing was going round and round and I was afraid of it clicking off. I turned it off but word for word what he said was in the Sunday Independent that weekend and it didn't come from me. I was shocked. I couldn't get over it. I know some players thought it was me but it wasn't and I never knew who it was.

Training was called for the Thursday night and when we got there nobody togged out. Henry Downey put it to Mickey – our captain and loyal as they come, 'I thought you weren't going to stay on here if the players didn't want you. It's obvious the players don't want you'. Mickey denied it. Fergal McCusker called him a fucking liar; Brian McCormick called him a lying cunt.

Another training session was called and only four players trained so other boys had to be brought in for the National League. Laois beat Derry by 18 points.

After that game and after the county board had eventually met Daddy, he met with the team in Ballymaguigan. Five weeks after his sacking, he told them that the Derry team and Derry football was bigger than Eamonn Coleman, bigger than Mickey Moran and told the players all to go back. There was a heated dispute, a lot of debate. Damien McCusker and them boys swore, 'No fucking way'. Daddy insisted but I wished he hadn't because I didn't want them to go back. I know he did the right thing because nobody could hold him responsible, but I wasn't for going back.

In my opinion, if Mickey had have backed him then we could have saved that great Derry team. If Mickey Moran had even said 'Right, the rest of the management team is stepping down in support of Eamonn Coleman' and let it go for a week or two then I'm sure the players would have said, 'We're a good team here; there's no point in us breaking up'. If they'd then realised that the county board wasn't going to let him back in, the players would have said 'Mickey and youse boys come in again' and everyone would have been 100% behind them. But it was the dirty, underhand deeds that destroyed it. Him being made manager the day before Daddy came home, it was all a total setup.

But Mickey was in and Daddy was out and I never came back until the following January. That first night in early '95, I went back to training in Owenbeg. Mickey was standing with Kieran McKeever and the physio and as I passed, he said goodnight. I walked straight past him but he followed me to the car and said, 'Don't you ever cut me off in front of people again'.

I hadn't cut him off but I'd no intentions of talking to him about anything else about football. I said, 'I'll not cause you any problems or give you any hassle but I don't have to be social to you.' He told me not to come back. I assured him, 'Oh don't worry Mickey, I'll be at training next week'.

Personally, I don't know what Mickey Moran expected. Did he expect me just to come in and go on as if nothing had happened? If he did then he was stupid because what other loyalties was I going to have? They treated Daddy very badly. But the lies and the small mindedness just never ceased and I wasn't in the form for putting up with it. Later when he told me to say nothing to the press I agreed, saying, 'I'll say nothing to nobody if you give me a fair crack'.

Training went on and I'd given no bother but I still hadn't spoke to him. I had played quite well in two friendlies we had before we were due to play Down at Celtic Park in the National League in February. There'd been eight to ten training sessions and I'd been to every one but that week I was going down to see Da who was living in Mullingar. I told Mickey I wouldn't be at the first training session but I'd be back for the second and he said that was ok.

In the Carrig Rua in Dungiven he named the panel and I wasn't on the team or the subs. I thought, 'This is bad' because I had trained real hard and he hadn't given me a fair crack. Liam Hayes phoned when I got home and said, 'Your name's not on the panel. Have you anything to say?'

I said, 'You're damned right I have' and I slagged Mickey Moran for his treatment of me. The Sunday Press then carried the article about me at home watching FA Cup games while Down were playing Derry.

The Tuesday night after training I was told to stay behind – that Dinny McKeever, Harry Gribben and Mickey Moran wanted to speak to me. Mickey came on about me talking to the press and just pure lied about me missing training. Dinny and Harry got laid in too but I didn't take if from any of them.

I challenged Mickey over promising me a fair chance only for him to leave me out of the squad. He claimed his answer to me was that if I went to Da's that I wouldn't be on the twenty-four for the Down match. I said, 'Mickey you're nothing but a fucking liar. Them two is going to back you to the hilt but you know and I know that's not what you said. I played well and you haven't given me a fair chance'.

He said, 'You played alright'. I turned to Dinny and asked, 'Why are you here? You're friends with our family this many a year. I mind you coming down to visit when I was only a youngster and now you're part of this?'

He called up about me going to the house after Daddy's sacking. 'Remember you told me not to get involved?' he said. 'Well when you left, I decided to get involved'. And then he proved what it really all come down to and that was getting the glory.

'Do you think Eamonn Coleman won Derry the All-Ireland?' Obviously they didn't. They thought it was a good team and it was just going to roll on but there's reasons for it being succesful. Everything has to be right; you have to have a good manager and they had got rid of him.

'He played one hell of a part in it, Dinny', I said, 'but if I'm going to be fair, Mickey was a good trainer and together they were a good team but Da was the man and everybody knows that.'

Harry had his say, 'What about the rest of us?' and 'What's your opinion of me, Gary?'

I thought, 'Oh my God, he's leaving himself wide open here', and I started, 'Well Harry, you're only a fucking ball pumper; balls and water that's all you're good for and I think you're only a cunt'.

'Well if I'm a cunt you're an even bigger cunt', he replied, just like a big child. There was nothing could be sorted out from it.

They kept me till after midnight that night and I had to go home for work the next day, upset. They held me back again one other night until after 11 pm until I said, 'To hell with this, I'm leaving'. Three of them and me and they were there to back each other up.

The whole year was a disaster. We trained away but there was no heart in the Derry team. We won the League in '95 and Tyrone beat us in the Ulster Semi-Final with thirteen men. If Tyrone had have had ten men, they'd have beaten us that day. That's how bad the whole thing was. It's not that boys weren't trying, it was just the whole year was a joke. The heart had been pulled right out of it. To me, people played for the sake of playing but there was no atmosphere and the spirit was terrible. It had taken a lot to make me go back but I was only twenty-one years of age and all I'd ever wanted to do was play for Derry. I'd won a National League and an All-Ireland and the past two years were class. I thought, 'This team is good; this team could win something again' and I didn't want not to be involved in it. I also felt that by not going back, I was giving them an easy ride. They were going to have to find an excuse not to pick me. When they couldn't find excuses, they started creating them and they kept me on the bench for three months. Mickey Moran eventually brought me on in the last minute against Cavan in the National League quarter-final, started me against Tyrone in the semi-final and then played me after that. But at the end of the year, when he decided to come back again, I said I would no longer play under him. I spoke to the papers, said the team was a joke and the Derry team would go no further under this management. Karl Diamond said much the same.

Mickey named his new panel in September '95. Two years after winning an All-Ireland medal and I wasn't on it. After calling two training sessions and only six people turned up, he saw it was over and resigned. Brian Mullins' appointment later that month was supposed to be the new start so a few of the boys said I should come up to training and keep in touch. I went up to Owenbeg and although I wasn't training, I was told by a man standing with Harry Chivers that I wasn't welcome. It was Mickey Moran's panel and until the new manager came in, I wasn't to show my face there.

When Brian Mullins came in, we had a meeting in Dungiven where he talked about leaving everything behind. But that also turned out to mean very little as I discovered after everyone had left. The county board was looking for my head for talking about Mickey Moran in the paper. Brian said I wouldn't be let play until it was sorted out, after he had stood up in front of the players with the message that everything was all over. 'You hadn't the guts to tell them it's not all over', I said. 'It would have been a different story if you had and you know that.' There was to be a meeting in Limavady but I had learned my lesson and wasn't going to go alone and took Henry Downey with me. The county board were looking to suspend me unless I offered an apology. I refused. After all that they put me through, what they put our family through, the way the county board had left it was open to slander. People were saying all sorts of things. That was the hurt they caused us and I wasn't going to apologise to them. That was far from the end of it. We were playing Armagh in the O'Fiaich cup and, standing in the changing room, Brian Mullins asked me for the apology. I said, 'I haven't got one and you'll not be getting one', so he took me into the shower area and said I wasn't going to play. Standing in the changing rooms ahead of the match I said, 'Don't be fucking stupid', but I wasn't allowed to tog out. Yet another county board meeting was called and I got slaughtered by the lot of them.

From the county chairman, Chivers, the county secretary, Patsy Mulholland, the entire members of the board, about my behaviour and my attitude and talking to the press. I gave no cheeky answers; the responses I gave were mannerly but the only man that stood up in the room and backed me was my former room-mate Richard Ferris, then a delegate from the North Derry board.

In the meantime, Karl Diamond had been playing away but they didn't seem to want to make anything of him. For me it was a different matter. Harry Gribben stood up and said, 'Does Gary think he owes the management an apology?'

I said that I didn't and I'd also heard Mickey Moran didn't want an apology. That's when things got really nasty. Mickey said, 'Mr Chairman, Gary's right I didn't want an apology but after what's happened lately I do. It's bad enough things are being said against me but when they are said against my family. Mr Chairman, my wife took a telephone call and the abuse she got down the phone was unbelievable.'

I stopped him in his tracks. I couldn't believe what he was saying and it was being directed towards me. I said, 'Mickey, I don't like you but I never would have thought of it. I think it's disgraceful somebody ringing your home and saying things to your wife or your family. It's totally against anything I would do but if you want to keep going down this road, I'll get a solicitor onto it.'

Then they started the same craic they had started with Da, half-baked accusations and leaving things hanging. He said he had heard that I had said things and demanded an apology. 'What was I supposed to have said?' I asked.

The county chairman replied, 'We cannot release those details.'

Personally, I felt let down by Brian Mullins because I sat in the room and took serious abuse and he never once interrupted. At training I'd been getting on well with Brian; there was nothing personal between me and him but I felt he let me down and I told him going back in the car. He didn't back me at all, I felt, and I was disappointed in him but I wouldn't hold it against him. There was enough of that going on.

They gave me two weeks to send in a written apology and still I refused so I was suspended for two weeks without giving any. Having not let me play February, March and half of April, I sat out my suspension and played my first game back in May '95. I got the last laugh by making full back for the final and got my National League medal for playing seventy minutes.

AFTERWORD
LOUGHSHORE LIFE, A CHILDHOOD
by Eamonn Coleman

I was as big at fourteen as I am now, physically. I didn't grow much more after that. But playing with Ballymaguigan seniors from that early age meant I grew up quickly. The death of my mother, Peggy, the year before had shortened my childhood as well, but I was protected as much as possible by my father and my sisters, Eileen and Mae. I had been just thirteen and they were so good, and it never was so bad because Eliza, my aunt, was always there.

My mother was a very jolly person, who'd have sat chatting for hours and if somebody had called she'd have never bothered about the tea. Small with long, black, curly hair, blue eyes and a kind face, she never would have ridiculed anybody and was all craic and smiles and fun. Her and my Da were very close and he would never have stopped her from getting anything.

She was mad about football and would run down the shore after the fishermen to get the local scores. In '60 and '61, Down was the big team and whenever they were playing she'd light the Blessed Candles and set them on the radio. The radio was a big thing for her and she always had it on for the football, radio plays and music. On the summer nights, she used to set it out on the street; you could have heard it across the fields.

I can remember her being sick and propped up in bed with pillows but that was because she had asthma – that was all I knew about it. But the summer before she died, she had been in great form and with everyone else away at work, it was just me and her. Eliza did all the heavy work for mammy was weak but I wasn't really aware of that until I was about nine or ten. Only that one summer of 1960, she was fit to go with Eliza to the lough. They'd have put two or three stones down, built a fire, set the bath on it to do the washing and the two of them talked for hours.

I had been in at the hospital the evening she died but she had sent me home for a football match. I hadn't a clue she was going to die. She'd been talking to me as usual although I overheard two women talking when I'd been sent out to the waiting room. One said, 'That woman Mrs Coleman must be very ill because she raved the whole night'. I didn't even know what they were talking about – raving – I thought her head was away or something.

I was at the football match when she died and the master came down to get me. Master Young came into the dressing room. Everybody was there after the game. 'Your mother's gone to heaven', was all he said. I didn't cry because I wanted to be a big boy in front of all the others. I never even cried when she was being buried. My Da cried often, on his own down the room. Mae and Eileen kissed her and touched her in the coffin, stroking her hair and that, but I couldn't. Then, a month or so after she died, I went to bed and cried half the night and that was really the only time I ever did. There was good times again alright but my father never was as jolly as he was when she was living. Him and her was that close. But it's not as bad at thirteen as it is at twenty, I think. It was harder for Eileen and Mae because they understood better what was going on.

She never got to see me play for the seniors but, of course, she knew I was mad about it but that wouldn't have been remarked on because that's what everyone did. It's football; that's what happened – it's just accepted in the community. You were either good or you were bad but you were at the football. I lived for football, nothing else mattered to me, nothing bothered me only getting to the football field. I would have played the whole day long.

Ballymaguigan were playing Ballerin in the 1957 county final and Mae was going to the match but I wasn't allowed to go as I was only nine years old. I had my Da's heart broke kicking football to him on a Sunday and he took me to my first match the following year in Ballinascreen. Beaten again in the county final, only this time against Bellaghy. The only team to win the county championship was the one I played on in '62.

My loyalties to Ballymaguigan were just what they were supposed to be – your own townland – but if I couldn't play with them anybody would do. At a carnival seven-a-side tournament in the late fifties, Ballymaguigan put out a team and at eleven or twelve years of age, I couldn't get on it. A team with men like Eddie and Frank McKeever was playing against Newbridge minors but Newbridge came with only five players so I got a game with them. We beat Ballymaguigan in the final and I got a ten-shilling prize. Sure, I was a millionaire.

At that stage, I'd have been playing schoolboy football for Ballinderry as Ballymaguigan hadn't an underage team. One Sunday I went with them to Portglenone at two o'clock to play on their schoolboy seven-a-side. Then we put in a minor seven-a-side and I played with them. Ballymaguigan landed with the senior seven-a-side at eight o'clock and I played with the seniors. We won the senior seven-a-side and lost the other two. That was as a schoolboy, but even when I started playing with the county, I only missed one match for Ballymaguigan in ten years.

Toome village, just round the shore from us, had a carnival every year in July and it was the big thing.

Packed with women, there was a beauty contest and if you played well in the carnival final you'd a good chance of leaving home the carnival queen. I left home several. There might have been 3000 at the game and a boy of fifteen or sixteen playing against men of thirty stood out. I would have been one of the good players; I'd have been quick and took the ball through but I took a lot of abuse and a lot of knocking down. When I was getting hit, I could hear the people, 'ouch' 'oooh', 'ahh'. A wee boy like me, they were feeling every dig and people got to know you that way too. I had been a quiet person and wouldn't have spoken to anybody much until I started going to football. By the time I was in my final year with the minors, in 1965 when we won the All-Ireland, I had come out of my shell but up until then I'd have been quite shy.

The minors would have had a healthy respect for me because I was playing senior at club level. Although there would have been a few playing senior like Malachy McAfee, Brendan Mullen and Colum Mullen from Ballerin, there was very few fourteen year olds playing senior football. As the youngest in Ireland ever to win a senior championship medal, it was a big record to have.

After that I started to go about with the senior players, Eddie McKeever and Frank McKeever and Joe McKee and them boys, who was all four or five years older than me so I was learning from, what to me, was experienced men.

Then if you were fit to make the county team, people would have made a point of speaking to you. I don't know if I ever thought about it but when I started to play on the senior team and went to dances, women would have knew you which always made you feel a bit better.

But football wasn't my first sporting passion. That was boxing. And Charlie Murphy, from that great Ballymaguigan football family who I'd have gone to every day after school, was into boxing. Charlie took me to the Kings Hall in Belfast to see Freddie Gilroy and John Caldwell in their epic bout in 1962. I went with Charlie and another man, Pat Mulholland, in the car; it was like going to England. I never was in Belfast in my life. The furthest I'd have been was Magherafelt, twice a year, once in the school holidays and at Christmas to see the crib and the highlight of that was getting a sixpenny ice cream in Agnew's shop. But getting to that fight in Belfast was another highlight of '62. They called Caldwell the Cold Eyed Killer but I was a Gilroy man. He won. Going into the Kings Hall and the fella outside was saying, 'Buy a photo of Bonnie Wee Freddie' – funny the things you remember.

There was a boxing club in Ballymaguigan and I wasn't too bad although I got plenty of slaps round the ears and got hammered several times. But I was looked on as one of the big boys because I was playing on the senior team. Even the ones round my age was thinking I was a big fella.

It never bothered me a bit, being amongst the men. I was just determined to prove myself playing senior football for Ballymaguigan. I'd have got nervous maybe as a manager before a big All-Ireland game at Croke Park but I never had a bit of fear on a football field in my life.

The only time I've been really afraid was when my daughter Margaret got sick just as she went into secondary school – the worst fear I ever had because I thought she had leukaemia. She was always with me, being a tomboy running about and playing football. Then for two weeks, she just lay down; she'd no energy or anything. It was a relief to hear at last that it was tuberculosis. The whole family had to be scanned and we found out that I'd had it myself as a youngster and had been able to fight it off. No one knew I had it until the scans showed it up on my lungs.

There was another incident when I was child that could have put an end to me and another that could have put an end to my football career. In the winter of 1950, a bad storm had come and my eldest sister Eileen took me down to the lough when my mammy and the rest were at second Mass. Nine years older than me, she'd wanted to walk out on the ice and as a babby, I was only too happy to follow her. The ice cracked and I went in but bobbed up once and she was able to grab me. The whole back of my neck was cut along the ice pulling me out. If she hadn't held onto me, I'd have been a goner. Just look at what the world would have missed!

The same sister took me up the lane to our grand uncle Paddy Mackle's house one time. He'd have had an open fire with the black tea stewing on it. I was about five years of age and pulled the tea round me, scalding my entire foot. I was that badly burned, I'd to be pushed about in an oul' pram, but I remember I quare played up on it.

We were a close, happy family. We were working class but there was nothing that any of us wanted. The things we needed we always got, for my father was a real hard worker.

He wasn't a farmer but he'd have kept a few cattle and we'd have had fifty or sixty pigs. He worked out all the time, whatever he could get – on the water piping and things like that. He took land over as you go into Magherafelt and would ride a bike in after work to put potatoes in. He put the garden in every summer, spuds and vegetables, and in winter he'd sell salt herrings. The boats on the lough wouldn't have been fishing so he'd take the horse and his spring cart and go round selling them.

Fishing was the industry; that's what the local people all lived on – eels and pollens and trout. Money was short and that's what was there, so that's what we ate.

My Da never fished. He'd have set an odd salmon net but he never went out at night fishing, but the house would have been full at night with all the fishermen from abouts, in here for the craic. If it had been blowing, they'd have stayed 'til the early hours, waiting for it to calm.

I had to feed the pigs in the evening and clean them out. There was no water so I'd have had to carry the water from the lough. And I had to dig the garden because I was a boy. I hated that but I'd no other choice.

We'd a big kitchen with a fire, a stove and a hearth and a big couch used to sit along the wall. The drinking water for the tea and the house had to be brought from Maggie Doyle's from the pump. Electricity didn't come until I was about twelve. We used a tilly lamp and then the gas and we kept warm around the fire. I can mind us all sitting around it and there'd always be people in, people come to listen to The McCooey's and The Kennedy's of Castleross and on Saturday nights, the ceili music.

My sisters were seven and nine years older than me so they were sort of beyond hanging about with and they didn't want me running about them because they thought they were big girls. But in the long winter's nights by the lough we had to make do with each other.

Eileen was a wicked little article, always looking to play nurses and stuff like that, giving you injections; she'd have tortured me and Mae. She'd have you lying down and her coming at you with a knitting needle to give you an injection and 'Do you want something to drink?' She'd have annoyed your happiness.

Mae was easier because she was just lazy and she'd have left you alone but she was a great fisherwoman and would have gone out setting nets on the boats. At fourteen or fifteen, the men used to pay her to row because she was big and strong. She was that strong, she was hard on the bikes – she'd have needed an iron bike; my da couldn't have kept her in them. There was a boy lived up the road, John Duff, who thought he was a great bike man and there wouldn't have been a big fancy racer in the country he wouldn't have got. He'd have been out, with his head down and his arse up, peddling along. Mae used to fly past him and he'd have got off and kicked the bike. Jesus, she could have pushed it along. She ran into a neighbour, Sean Young, when he was in the car and she did more damage to the car than it did to her.

But the people that grew up around you was like family and all we wanted was to get out in the morning to go to the lough or the football field or to meet up with the McErlains or somebody else. Then there was Jim Lee and Bridget Lee and Ann Harvey and myself. The master, Master Mackle, used to call us 'the adopted twins'. He was on the Castledawson team we beat in the '62 final. Beating my schoolmaster in the final, that was great. We came in the next day and had two days celebrating until he said on the Tuesday evening, 'Come in tomorrow prepared to work'.

I wasn't interested in school work – I wasn't clever enough to be interested, but I absolutely loved school and even stayed over the time that I should have. The craic was good and I liked geography and religion. The Bible stories was brilliant; I'd only have heard them once and I'd have been able to remember them. If you had got anything for religion, I'd have been top of the class but although I went to Mass every morning in Lent, it was just an excuse to get out. It was the same for going to devotions every Sunday evening but oh Jesus, I hated the holy hour, an hour's praying that was more like an interrogation. My parents were deadly religious and the Rosary was said in the house every night and when you'd come in in the evening, my mother would be sitting with the prayer book open on her lap. You could tell by looking at her she meant and believed what she was doing.

I said my own prayers when I went to bed and when I woke up every morning. When I was going out to work, I'd leave the house at 6.50 am to get the bus at the crossroads. From when I closed the door, I ran to the school crossroads and every morning I said my prayers. It's not that it meant that much to me but it was the way I was brought up. I don't pray anymore except on Sunday when I go to Mass. I still go to Mass because I wouldn't feel right if I didn't. I believe in the hereafter but I don't believe you're judged by going to Mass or anything; you're judged by the way you live your life. I still go to Mass because I always went to Mass and I go to pray for my mother and father.

Mind you, it wasn't the first time I cried when my mother died. I cried like a cuddy after my da beat the shit out of me for not coming home from the football field. I was to be home at nine o'clock and Eliza had his head around the bend about where I was. He lay into me with a stick. I can mind me curling up on the big couch to try and save myself. I only got two hammerings in my life and that was one of them and the second one was for doing the same thing. If he'd have known half the things I was up to, he'd have killed me: sodding people on bikes, scaring the life out of people in their houses by standing up on Jim Lee's shoulders with a big coat round us and pretending to be a giant man. Even when I had started work, me and Jim Lee would have been messing. On our way out of town on a Saturday evening, we started leaving squibs on Dennis McKeever's window sill then knocking at the door and running off. He didn't know who it was, so this night, he hid and waited for us. He darted out, I made to run and he stuck out his foot to trip me. I went for about twenty yards off balance then I straightened up and away. He said, 'I fucking knew it was you then Eamonn, for you were fit to keep on your feet.'

That was our great fun on a Saturday night even when I was working age. My da wanted me to be a motor mechanic for he knew a man that could get me a start. But when I was about sixteen, a local man, Barney O'Neill, was building a chimney for my da at the house. I was up in the roof and I liked the height so I decided to be a bricklayer. I started a couple of weeks after that. Being a mechanic was too dirty for me; I was a clean wee boy and didn't like getting my hands dirty like that.

It didn't bother my da at all. He was just glad I had work but he gave me a bag like you go shopping with for my tools and I was embarrassed having to carry it to work.

I would have loved to have been a professional footballer. I think it's a shame that people can't be professional footballers in the GAA but there's not enough money in it; it's too localised. They couldn't afford to pay club players. They could maybe afford county players but that would cause trouble too. I wouldn't be into paying for playing football beyond giving expenses and looking after players when they get injured. Have their money there on a Friday evening and then when the insurance money comes, the county board can take it out of that. I don't believe a player should be going two months without getting money.

Everybody thinks I get a pile of money. No one believes, even Derry people, that I get 30p a mile. I never got money out of it and I don't know why people thinks that. Anybody that knows Derry football knows they don't pay money.

So now I'm just going to enjoy going to football. There's no pressure on me, just people saying, 'What do you think, what do you think?'– Like Tyrone ones – and I'll say, 'Ah Tyrone's a great team'; Tyrone ones love you to say that. There's a fella from Tyrone working round here and he said to me, 'You know, Eamonn, up in Tyrone they hate you with a passion but you're not a bad fella'. I said, 'You know this, you're right, but I get more satisfaction out of beating Tyrone than of any other team in the country'. He just laughed.

ACKNOWLEDGEMENTS

Acknowledgment and thanks are due to many people throughout the various stages of this project which began as Eamonn's autobiography back in 2002.

I owe a special debt of gratitude however to those who have helped ensure this publication as a memoir of his All-Ireland triumph, twenty-five years on.

For fact checking, proofreading and contributions, I would like to thank Joe Brolly, Enda Gormley, Adrian McGuckin, Gary Coleman, my brothers Martin, John and Christopher McCourt and Patricia Mulvenna Doyle. Also, for agreeing to turn this book around in an insanely short period of time, publisher Conor Graham and managing editor Fiona Dunne of Irish Academic Press/Merrion Press.

Photographs are courtesy of *The Irish News*, with special thanks to Ann McManus and Hugh Russell, as well as Derry GAA photographer Danny B. O'Kane. Thanks also to Danny and to Enda Gormley for the book loans and guidance.

ACKNOWLEDGEMENTS

Connla Young and Mal McCann deserve a special mention for both their practical and personal support as do Eamonn's children, Margaret, Gary and Vivian.

The lasting treasure of Eamonn's triumphs is that they were shared by us all as a family and I would like to take this opportunity to also acknowledge my sister Bernadette and the wider McCourt, McMullan and Mulvenna clanns; the O'Neill and O'Hara families, kin by another name; Colette and the O'Reilly and McGahern families in Gowna, Co. Cavan.

Finally, to Eamonn whose loss looms large: for the friendship and the craic, and for trusting me to do this. The words are his, errors or omissions are mine.

Maria McCourt, September 2018